the yoga sutras of patanjali

the yoga sutras
of patanjali

illuminated

gary kissiah

second edition

Lilalabs

Pada Three: Vibhuti Pada

Introduction

I believe that every student of Yoga
should not only read but actually study
the Yoga Sutra(s).
It is an excellent way of delving into the
metaphysics and the spiritual practice of Yoga.
All too often, Western students want to
bypass the philosophical aspects of Yoga
and go on with its practice.
But it is impossible to practice
Yoga authentically without first having
grasped its metaphysics.

Georg Feuerstein

My Journey to the Yoga Sutras

As a student of Yoga for over fifteen years I have taken classes from many different teachers in the United States and India. Even though I gained many important insights from all of my teachers, I found that most of my classes concentrated heavily on asana. As my practice progressed, I became interested in exploring the great questions of Yoga philosophy that are rarely discussed in Yoga classes. Where did we come from? Where are we going? Why is there something rather than nothing? What is my true Self, and how does practicing Yoga help me find it? What do I get when I realize my true Self, anyway? What is the cause of suffering, and how does Yoga end suffering? All of these questions are explored with depth and sophistication in Yoga philosophy, and I wanted some answers.

As I began my study of Yoga philosophy, I discovered an ocean of literature that has evolved over 5000 years. Much of this literature is highly complex, wrapped in mystery, and concerned with the human condition as it existed thousands of years ago in India. I found the writings difficult to understand without relying upon scholarly commentary. The scholarly commentary, in turn, was often as complicated as the source text. I realized that I did not know where to start in my exploration of Yoga philosophy. I had become lost in the complexity and vastness of the tradition.

During that time, I enrolled in the Yoga Philosophy Program offered by the California Institute of Integral Studies. We studied many great works of Yoga philosophy, including the Yoga Sutras. I learned that the Yoga Sutras are one of the most important works on Yoga and that the Sutras are a manual for understanding both the philosophy and practice of Yoga. When we chanted the Sutras in class, I was touched by their power and beauty and the way that the chants opened my heart. I decided to focus my exploration of Yoga philosophy on the Yoga Sutras and to use them as the foundation upon which I would compare and understand other systems of Yoga philosophy.

The Yoga Sutras were written in Sanskrit, an ancient language used in India for religious and scholastic purposes as early as 1500 BCE. The Sutras were written during 200–300 CE. The word *sutra* means to thread or to sew. In ancient times, sutra was used literally because the texts were written down on palm leaves that were sewn together with thread. In the context of the Sutras, it means a thread of words (some sutras are only two or three words long) that conveys meaning in a concentrated form. Because the Sutras contain deep insights into the most complex questions of Yoga philosophy and are highly condensed and technical, the use of a separate commentary is essential.

However, many of the commentaries on the Sutras are academic, difficult to understand, and assume the reader's knowledge of Sanskrit and Yoga philosophy. The commentaries vary enormously in their translation of the Sanskrit text and level of discourse. For any given sutra, it is possible to find very different translations and divergent views on its meaning. The difficulty of studying the Sutras is compounded because they do not contain poetic imagery, myth, or stories like other wisdom texts, such as the Bhagavad Gita, the Bible or the Tao Te Ching. Even though I approached my study of the Sutras with a great deal of dedication, I found it difficult to reach even a rudimentary level of understanding, to relate the Sutras to my personal practice, and to find their relevance to modern life. Many of my fellow students shared similar experiences when they attempted to study the Sutras.

After I began my study of Yoga philosophy, I took a sabbatical to India to deepen my Yoga practice. I studied at Parmarth Niketan in Rishikesh. Every evening as the sun set over the Ganga River, crowds of people gathered on the steps leading to the water's edge in front of the ashram where Pujya Swami Chidanand Saraswati led the arati ceremony. He describes it as follows:

Arati is the beautiful ceremony in which deepas (the oil lamps) are offered to God. Arati can be done for a deity in the temple, it can be done on the banks of the Ganges for Mother Ganga, or it can be done for a saint. It is performed for God, in any manifestation, any form, by any name. The essence of the arati ceremony is that all day long God offers us light—the light of the sun, the light of life, the light of His (Her) blessings. Arati is a time when we say, "Thank you," and we offer back the light of our thanks, the light of our love, and the light of our devotion. We realize that the small deepa is nothing compared to the divine light, which shines on us all day. So, arati is

*a ceremony of humility, a time in which we acknowledge that God,
You are everything. I am nothing. All day You shine upon the world.
All I can offer You is this small deepa, a flame, which will be blown
out by the passing wind. But, I offer it with devotion and with love.
Please accept my offering.*

I will never forget the image of the flickering candles floating down
the Ganges in their little boats made of leaves, the ritual fire offered
by the priests and the sound of the people sitting on the steps and
chanting. As darkness fell, I became inspired to write a book on the
Sutras that would take a new approach to unpacking their meaning.
The book would use imagery to bring the Sutras to life and provide
an inviting entry into this great ancient wisdom.

In the spirit of the arati ceremony, I am offering this book with humility. The Yoga Sutras are complex and attaining any deep understanding of the Sutras is a lifelong practice. Many spiritual masters and
scholars have written commentaries on the Sutras; I cannot hope to
attain their level of insight. In fact, B. K. S. Iyengar, in the introduction to his book *Light on the Yoga Sutras of Patanjali* remarked that
he would need several lifetimes to plumb the depths of the Sutras!
Nonetheless, if my book encourages you to begin your study of the
Sutras, then it will have served its purpose.

The Origins of Patanjali and the Yoga Sutras

The Yoga Sutas are comprised of 196 sutras organized into four
chapters. These chapters are the Padas. The first Pada is known as
the Samadhi Pada, the second as the Sadhana Pada, the third as the
Vibhuti Pada and the fourth as the Kaivalya Pada.

Although there is a fair amount of debate on the date the Sutras were written, the consensus among the scholars is that they were written during 200-300 CE by Patanjali. Although very little is known historically about Patanjali, his origins are described in Hindu mythology.

Before Patañjali was born, Vishnu was lying upon his couch-the serpent Lord Adisesa- watching Shiva dance. Vishnu was so moved by the dance that his body began to vibrate with the rhythm of the dance and he became heavier and heavier. This caused Adisesa great discomfort. When the dance ended, Vishnu's body became light again. When Adisesa asked Vishnu what had happened, Vishnu explained that the beauty and grace of Shiva's dance created vibrations in his body that made it heavy. Adisesa then decided he wanted to learn to dance so that he could perform for Vishnu's pleasure. Vishnu was impressed and predicted that one day Shiva would bless Adisesa for his devotion. His desire to dance would be fulfilled, and he would be incarnated in human form to bestow humanity with blessings.

Adisesa began to meditate to find out who would be his future earthly mother. At the same time, a virtuous woman named Gonika was praying for a son. She felt that her earthly life was ending, but she had not yet found a son to whom she could pass on the wisdom gained through her Yoga practice. She prayed to the Sun God to bring her a son. She scooped up a handful of water, meditated upon the Sun God, and prepared to present her offering. Seeing this, Adisesa knew that he had found his mother.

Just as Gonika was about to offer her handful of water to the Sun God, she glanced down at her hands and was astonished to see a tiny serpent moving in her hands. She became even more astonished when, within a few moments, the serpent assumed a human form. Adisesa asked her to accept him as her son. This she happily did and named him Patanjali. *Pata* means falling in Sanskrit and *anjali* means hands folded in prayer. Thus, Gonika's prayer with folded hands depicts the name Patanjali, who became the author of the Yoga Sutras.

A New Path to Understanding the Yoga Sutras

The facts of higher Yoga can neither be proved nor demonstrated. Their appeal is to the intuition and not to the intellect.
I. K. Taimni

The Sutras do not use stories or poetry to give us an easy pathway into understanding their meaning. They read like a dry scientific treatise on the subject of the transformation of consciousness. My inspiration at Rishikesh was to use imagery, commentary, and book design to illuminate the Sutras and bring them to life. The commentaries and quotations that I selected for the Sutras are from a wide range of wisdom traditions as well as spiritual and academic authorities.

Although I do not want to diminish the importance of understanding the Sutras from an intellectual point of view, I feel that a complete understanding of the Sutras must also include the perspective of art, emotion and the heart. The goal of Yoga is to reside in our true Self. Because this state transcends the experience of our ordinary minds, it cannot be described in words or understood by intellectual analysis. It can only be experienced through the heart.

Nischala Joy Devi describes a heart-centered perspective on the Sutras in her book *The Secret Power of Yoga* as follows:

For many years I've been a student of the Yoga Sutras. I've sought to understand them from a "rational" view. This striving relaxed as the "heart perspective" invited itself into my study. Embracing the spirit of the sutras, rather than their literal meaning, allows me to integrate the sacred teachings at a much deeper level. In a way, it is like bypassing the mind and going directly to the heart and soul. This allowed me to "feel" the vibration of what is meant.

I hope that my approach to the Sutras will help you experience them with both your heart and your mind, enabling you to appreciate the richness of their worldview, their insights into Yoga practice and philosophy, and their practical wisdom for living in the modern world.

Practicing the Yoga Sutras

How does the modern Yoga student approach the study and practice of the Yoga Sutras? What relevance does this ancient work have to our lives and Yoga practice in the 21st century? How can it guide us as we navigate the freeways to the office, the demands of living in a digital world, and the economic and physical stresses inherent in modern society?

In ancient India, the teachers used a threefold method of teaching spiritual wisdom: *sravana, manana* and *nididhyasana*. Sravana is listening to a sacred text as it is chanted or spoken by the teacher. Manana is logical reflection on the meaning of the text, and nididhyasana is absorbing the text through practice and experience.

In the spirit of the traditional teaching method, I believe that approaching the Sutras from several different perspectives is an effective way to learn them and to integrate them into your practice.

First, you can chose a sutra that relates to your Yoga practice or to a problem or dilemma that you face in your life. I have found that selecting one of the *yamas* or *niyamas* (i.e., the great vows and observances) is good for this purpose. After you have selected a sutra, study it and then keep it in your mind throughout the course of your day.

As Sri Swami Satchidananda says, "Study them slowly and carefully, and meditate on them. You can even learn some of the most important and useful ones by heart." It may be helpful to write the sutra on a note card and keep it with you. By reflecting on the sutra throughout the day, you may find that it keeps you centered and provides new insights into your daily life.

I recommend the following sutras to start your studies:

SUTRA 1.12
Restriction of the fluctuations is achieved by practice and non-attachment.

SUTRA 1.29
From this practice (meditation on OM), obstacles disappear, and the true Self is realized.

SUTRA 1.33
The mind becomes tranquil through the practice of friendliness toward the happy, compassion toward the miserable, joy toward the virtuous, and equanimity toward the non-virtuous.

SUTRA 1.39
Consciousness becomes calm and serene by meditating on any desirable object that is spiritually uplifting.

SUTRA 2.30-2.31

The yamas are the great universal vows. They are not limited by place, time, or class. The yamas are non-violence, truthfulness, non-greed, non-stealing, and moderation.

SUTRA 2.35

In the presence of one who is established in non-violence, all hostility ends.

SUTRA 2.42

Contentment brings supreme happiness.

SUTRA 2.46

The posture should be steady and comfortable.

As we have seen, spiritual wisdom was traditionally taught orally; the sutra form made it easier for students to memorize their lessons. I have found chanting to be a powerful way to integrate the sutras into my practice. Chanting will not only help you remember the sutras but also connect you to the Sanskrit language and the oral tradition through which the Yoga Sutras were originally taught.

Chanting is also an important Yoga practice. In his commentary on Sutra 1.28, Sri Swami Satchidananda states: "Here we come to the practice of japa (i.e., chant). It is a very powerful technique and at the same time the easiest, simplest, and the best. Almost every religion advocates the repetition of God's name because all prophets, sages, and saints experienced and understood its greatness, glory and power." I have listed some resources for chants in the "Footnotes and Credits" at the end of this book.

After each block of sutras, I have left space for journal entries to help you capture your thoughts as you reflect on the sutras in your individual studies.

Many readers have told me that they like to read a sutra right before they fall asleep. This practice leads to restful sleep and may provide insights into the meaning of a sutra or resolving a problem.

In writing this book, I relied upon many books and resources that are listed in the "Footnotes and Credits." I would like to highlight the following books because they offer excellent insights into the Sutras and are approachable for beginning students:

Jaganath Carrera, *Inside the Yoga Sutras: A Comprehensive Sourcebook for the Study and Practice of Patanjali's Yoga Sutras* (Integral Yoga Publications, 2006).

Nischala Joy Devi, *The Secret Power of Yoga—A Woman's Guide to the Heart and Spirit of the Yoga Sutras* (Three Rivers Press, 2007).

Sri Swami Satchidananda, *The Yoga Sutras of Patanjali* (Integral Yoga Publications, 1978).

Edwin Bryant, *The Yoga Sutras of Patanjali* (North Point Press, 2009).

Swami Prabhavananda and Christopher Isherwod, *The Yoga Aphorisms of Patanjali* (Vedanta Society of Southern California, 1953).

On Navigation and the Icons

One of the difficulties that most readers of the Sutras encounter is navigating Patanjali's philosophical system. Almost all of the commentaries present the Sutras as a single body of work divided into the four main chapters, or Padas. This encourages a linear progression through the Sutras, and the tendency is to get lost by either going too deeply into a single sutra or reading the text too quickly without understanding the core concepts or the relationships among the sutras. This problem is aggravated by the fact that the Sutras are written in Sanskrit, densely packed with meaning, and the English translations are only loose equivalents of the Sanskrit language.

In my experience, the Sutras are best learned by exploring select groups of sutras with common themes that relate to your personal interests. As you study the groups of sutras, you can begin to see how they relate to your life, and they will become more and more meaningful to you over time. You will begin to see the deep connections among the sutras, and additional avenues of understanding and exploration will begin to open.

To provide a map for navigating the Sutras, I have organized them in thematic groups. These groups generally follow the system developed by Veda-Vyasa in his commentary on the Yoga Sutras, the *Yoga Bhashya*, which was written in 650-850 CE. By organizing the sutras in this way, it is easier to understand their broad themes. At the beginning of each of the groups, I provide a brief introduction to the main ideas expressed in the group.

As you study the Sutras, you will also find that key themes are repeated throughout the book but presented from different perspectives. Patanjali did this to accommodate practitioners at different levels of understanding Yoga philosophy and practice.

I have grouped the Sutras into eight loosely connected themes, and each sutra within that group has been given an icon that is associated with one of the eight themes. The icons are located below the sutra in each of the text blocks that contain the sutra and its quote. My hope is that this will help you to see the connections among the broad themes of the Sutras.

On the Images

The images were drawn from a wide variety of sources. Some of them are photographs I took on my travels through India, Nepal, Tibet, Indonesia, Europe, California, and New Mexico. Other images are in the public domain and were obtained from libraries, museums, and other archival sources. Each image was carefully selected to illuminate the meaning of its corresponding sutra.

On the Translation

There are several difficulties inherent in translating the Yoga Sutras. First, they were written in Sanskrit. Sanskrit is an ancient language of great subtlety and precision. It was codified by Panini in 500 BCE, and it has not changed since that time. Not only is Sanskrit a precise language, its sounds consist of vibrational harmonies that directly affect the energies of the human system. For this reason, the Sutras were intended to be learned by chanting them in the original Sanskrit. Vyaas Houston elegantly describes this:

The fluid nature of Sanskrit lends itself to easy memorization. Each individual sutra being like a hologramatic segment, the overall perspective begins to gel just having learned one. The one links by way of sound continuity and philosophical context to the next and likewise that to the next. If one conceives the project as a quantitative one for the mind, it will tend to be abandoned. The number of sutras, 196, is more than most minds can deal with. A sutra can only be learned, one at a time. Each one must literally be learned "by heart," an act of devotion to my true self, with a love for clarity and power of the truth being conveyed as well as the exquisite sounds it is conveyed through.

Any translation of the Sutras is complicated by the fact that there are no exact English equivalents for many of the Sanskrit words. The Sutras, by their very nature, are brief phrases and rarely use verbs. They are incomprehensible without extensive commentaries that explain their meaning; however, the commentaries vary widely in their interpretation.

My translation is intended to render the Sutras into plain English, using modern sentence structure, yet to remain accurate. I studied over twenty different translations of the Sutras and used the consensus of the authorities to determine the most accurate translation to use.

Finally, please note that my translation ends at Sutra 3.5. This is because Pada Two does not discuss all eight limbs of Patanjali's system of Astanga Yoga. The remaining three limbs-concentration (*dharana*), meditation (*dhyana*) and absorption (*samadhi*)—are treated in Sutras 3.1–3.5. Although the remainder of Pada Three and Pada Four are important, much of it is highly esoteric and so is of little interest to most Yoga students. Most of the masterworks cited above do address these sections, but in an abbreviated manner.

Acknowledgements

I would like to thank the many Yoga teachers, students, and friends who have helped me along the spiritual path and in writing this book. I want to extend a special thank you to Reverend Prem Anjali of Satchidananda Ashram-Yogaville for her inspiration, support and kindness in helping me write this book, as well as providing permission to use the writings of Sri Swami Satchidananda. I also want to express my gratitude to Swami Ramananda of the Integral Yoga Institute of San Francisco who gave me the courage to begin teaching Yoga philosophy and provided me with much guidance and support.

I want to recognize and honor the artistry of Ken Adams. His beautiful and complex imagery resonates spirituality and wisdom on many different levels, and his critical eye, assistance, and support have been invaluable to me in writing this book.

I want to acknowledge Bob Aufuldish and Kathy Warinner for creating the gorgeous book design and cover as well as their patience in working though my endless comments. The beauty of the book design alone has invited many students to begin their study of the Yoga Sutras.

Vesela Simic provided me with expert editorial support for this book and proved to me that you should never attempt to edit your own work!

Special thanks go to Sally Kempton, Jennifer Prugh, Jackie Dumaine, Daniella Cotreau, Carlos Pomeda, Mariana Caplan, Rachel Meyer, and Ashleigh Sergeant. Each of you has been a source of inspiration and support and I appreciate it greatly.

I would also like to recognize the following institutions that have helped me go deeper into spirit: Satchidananda Ashram-Yogaville in Buckingham, Virginia; Parmarth Niketan in Rishikesh, India; Esalen Institute in Big Sur, California; Tassajara Zen Center in Big Sur, California; Breathe Yoga in Los Gatos, California; Integral Yoga Institute in San Francisco, California; and Jivamukti Yoga in New York, New York.

Last, I want to acknowledge the support and patience of my beautiful wife Pam, as I spent many long nights and weekends in the Lilalabs Studio studying the Yoga Sutras and writing this book.

Samadhi Pada

Samadhi is seeing the soul face to face,
an absolute, indivisible state of existence,
in which all differences between body,
mind and soul are dissolved.

B. K. S. Iyengar

The first chapter of the Yoga Sutras is the Samadhi Pada. It is concerned with the practice and the state of samadhi. In fact, Vyasa, the first and most famous commentator on the Sutras, said that Yoga is samadhi.

Samadhi means "placing or putting together." The things that are "placed together" are the subject and the object. The mind is the subject. We view the objects of the world as separate from ourselves. We view the world as if we are inside of our heads looking through our eyes at an external reality. Everything is "out there." This type of awareness is known as dual thinking, and it is the ordinary way in which we perceive the world and our place in it. It leads to alienation between ourselves and nature, and ourselves and other people.

Samadhi is a radical shift in awareness; it is the state of union with the source, the ground of all being and the divine. In samadhi, the boundaries between subject and object, and inside and outside are dissolved. We merge into the source as the drop of water merges with the ocean. This is known as non-dual awareness. We can exist in a state of samadhi as we move through the world in our daily lives. The wisdom that comes from realizing samadhi helps us lead a more peaceful and joyous life. As Pujaya Swamiji said:

Samadhi means that we have the reins of our lives only in our own hands, we cannot be switched on and off like lightbulbs by other people. We know that we are one with God and that one-ness fills us with such peace, bliss and stability that nothing else can affect us. Samadhi means, essentially, that our lives are lived in peace, not in pieces, and that is the ultimate goal of Yoga-Divine Union.

Because this state is beyond the intellect and conceptual thinking, we cannot describe it in words. We can only experience the state of samadhi through our heart center which resides at a level deeper than the ego. In samadhi, we go beyond ordinary thought and experience the calm and quiet of our true nature. We are free from our ordinary thinking mind with all of its anxieties, conflicts and cares. We experience pure non-dual awareness. Because samadhi is such a profoundly expansive mode of awareness, it leads to Yogic wisdom.

In Sutra 1.2, Patanjali defined Yoga in just four words: "yoga citta vrtti nirodhah." This sutra may be translated as "Yoga is the cessation of the misidentification with the modifications of the mind." Sutra 1.3 states that we reside in our true nature when we silence our minds. The two sutras read together mean that we experience our true nature only when our minds become still and calm. This is the state of samadhi or non-dual awareness. Sutra 1.4 goes on to say that when we are not residing in our true nature, we become absorbed in the thing that is causing our minds to become unstable and agitated. In Pada One, Patanjali gave us many meditation practices to calm our minds and to reach samadhi.

Patanjali describes the qualities of right practice. Right practice is consistent, devoted, and joyous. However, right practice is non-attachment to the results of the practice. Although these two attitudes may appear paradoxical, we need both to successfully practice Yoga. In the same way, a bird needs two wings to fly.

The Definition of Yoga—
Yoga Citti Vrtti Nirodha

In the beginning was only Being, One without a second. Out of himself he brought forth the cosmos and entered into everything in it. There is nothing that does not come from him. Of everything he is the inmost Self. He is the truth; he is the Self supreme. You are That, Svetaketu; you are That.

The Chandogya Upanishad, Chapter 6, Verses 2.2–2.3

The living word or pure Consciousness—you are That.
The reflection of the King's face—you are That.
There is nothing outside of yourself, look within.
Everything you want is there—you are That.

Rumi

The great teaching of the Indian wisdom traditions is that everything in the universe-the stars, the sun, the sky, the earth, human beings, and all other forms of matter-is a manifestation of divine consciousness. This consciousness cannot be described in words nor analyzed by the intellect. It cannot be seen nor heard nor touched. Although different traditions refer to this consciousness using such names as God, Brahman, Purusha, Buddha-mind, Tao, or Spirit, it is beyond description. Because it is human nature to think of the divine in some way that we can understand, we may describe its qualities as satchidananda-being, consciousness, and bliss.

These eternal truths were revealed directly to the rishis by the Vedic gods. The rishis were the sages of ancient India, who received these truths and transmitted them to mankind. Some scholars have described the rishis as poets whose writings reflect their experiences of divine consciousness. The rishis embodied these truths in the Vedas. They did not create the Vedas but rather received eternal truths that already existed at the dawn of time.

The Vedas are the earliest sacred texts of ancient India. They are the fountain from which all of Indian culture and philosophy has flowed. The Vedas contain mantras, hymns to the Vedic gods, rituals, and expressions of awe for the gods and nature. The essential truth of the Vedas is that the universe is an endless dance of form, which is the manifestation of the divine. The Rig Veda proclaims that "Truth is one though the wise call it by many names."

The Upanishads are the last chapters of the Vedas. The word *upanishad* means "sitting down near," and it suggests a student sitting at the feet of a great teacher. The Vedas are more concerned with outward-facing rituals and hymns to the gods, whereas the Upanishads are concerned with inward-looking practices to directly experience divine consciousness.

The Upanishads teach three truths: (1) the divine being is the essence of all forms; (2) this divine being is the same as our true Self; and (3) we can realize our true Self directly, which is the meaning of life. Our true Self is the same as divine consciousness. At our deepest level, we are divine. As Svetaketu was taught by his father, in the Chandogya Upanishad: "You are That."

We find these same ideas expressed in the Yoga Sutras. The Yoga Sutras say that when we still our minds, we rest in our true nature or true Self. Yoga allows us to experience the wisdom of our true Self so that we may be guided by it to live with more freedom, peace and happiness.

You may have experienced your true Self in those rare moments when your everyday mind- with all of its conflicts, anxieties, fantasies, and projections- became quiet. This may have been triggered by an experience in a temple, in meditation, or in a Yoga class. You may have seen the world with crystalline clarity and experienced the dissolution of the boundary between your ordinary self and the natural world "out there." You may have had the sensation of the perfection of the world and felt peace, bliss and expansiveness, if only for a moment. This experience was a glimpse of your true Self.

Ken Wilber describes it this way: "In front of you, the clouds parade by, your thoughts parade by, bodily sensations parade by, and you are none of them. You are the vast expanse of freedom through which all these objects come and go. You are an opening, a clearing, an emptiness, a vast spaciousness, in which all these objects come and go."

However, these experiences are temporary because our ordinary mind inevitably returns, the internal monologue begins once again, and that pure moment of experiencing our true Self is lost.

It is as if our everyday minds are the clouds and the true Self is the sun. Even though we may not see the sun on a cloudy day, it is always shining. Because we are not united with our true Self, we do not have access to our natural state of light, unity, and bliss.

It is very difficult to experience our true Self because we habitually identify with the external world, our egoic minds, and our bodies. We see a world of multiplicity, impermanence, and duality. Consequently we often feel alone, disconnected, and alienated. The result is suffering.

According to Yoga philosophy, the basic reason we experience suffering is spiritual ignorance or *avidya*. Avidya is one of the key concepts that we will encounter throughout our exploration of the Sutras. Avidya is the fundamental misunderstanding of our true nature. It means we regard the impermanent as permanent, the impure as pure, the painful as pleasurable, and the non-self as the true Self. We identify with the endless fluctuations of our minds and with our bodies. This is avidya.

We know that the world, our minds, and our bodies are impermanent and constantly changing. We can easily see this in the changing of the seasons, the daily weather patterns, and the aging process in our own bodies. Yet, we avoid accepting change and attach ourselves to various illusions of permanence and stability because of avidya. We tend to grasp the world tightly because it provides us with a sense of security and peace but this only leads to suffering.

We have all sought happiness in material possessions only to find they inevitably become broken, out of style, or burdensome, and our happiness changes into frustration and emptiness. We then seek to acquire more possessions to regain our feeling of happiness, and the cycle continues. As Sri Ramana Maharshi said: "What happiness can you get from anything extraneous to yourself? When you get it, how long will it last?" When we identify with our everyday minds, we will never find peace because we will become entangled in the mind's endless conflicts and knots. When we are in this state, we cannot experience our true Self, and we suffer.

However, through our Yoga practice, we can gain spiritual wisdom. This is known as *viveka*. As we gain spiritual wisdom, we begin to overcome spiritual ignorance and may experience our true Self.

In Yoga Sutra 1.2, Patanjali defines Yoga as "citta vrtti nirodha." This sutra may be translated as "Yoga is the cessation of the misidentification with the modifications of the mind." This is one of the most important and well-known sutras because it defines Yoga in just four words. Let's briefly explore each of these key words.

Citta comes from the Sanskrit root word *cit* which means "to observe, to perceive or to know." It is usually translated as the "mind," but it refers to all three levels of the mind: *buddhi* (wisdom and discrimination), *ahamkara* (ego), and *manas* (intellect).

Vrtti comes from the Sanskrit root word *vrt* which means "to turn, to whirl or to revolve." It is often translated "fluctuations or modifications." Patanjali uses vrtti to describe both the content and the activity of our everyday minds. Our minds are in a constant state of activity as they process experiences, emotions, conflicts, anxieties, attachments, and aversions. Even though some of these activities may be experienced as pleasant or beneficial, they are still vrtti activities.

If we consider our everyday experiences, we can observe the activities of the vrttis at work. What does it take to disturb the peaceful, relaxed, and open mind we attain on the yoga mat? The slow driver blocking our lane on the highway, the phone call from work on our day off, a broken dinner date, a rainy day that ruins a hike we planned in the mountains? Suddenly we lose our center, we become out of sorts, and we react negatively and inappropriately throughout the rest of the day. This is vrtti activity.

We naturally identify with the vrtti activities because that is the way we ordinarily experience, interpret, and interact with the world. As a result of this, our true Self is obscured and forgotten, and we experience ourselves as impermanent and isolated beings. We lose our inner peace. Reverend Jaganath Carrera describes this as follows: "Identification with vritti activity obscures our experience of the true Self. It takes us away from the objective truth of pure experience and involves us in the drama of the mind—the dance of light and shadow that is vritti activity." In Yoga philosophy, this misidentification with the whirl of the vrttis is the result of spiritual ignorance and the cause of suffering.

The ultimate goal of Yoga is to end our identification with the vrttis. When this occurs, we naturally reside in our true Self because it is there all along; it is just obscured or veiled by the vrttis. But how are we to accomplish the goal? The key lies in *nirodha*.

Nirodha means "cessation," and it refers to the process of ending our misidentification with the activities of the vrttis and the effect they have on us. This occurs through the practice of Yoga.

Sutra 1.3 states that when the vrttis are completely restrained, we experience our true Self. Conversely, Sutra 1.4 states that when the vrttis are active, our mind becomes identified with the vrttis, so we cannot experience the true Self.

Reverend Jaganath Carrera explains:

Vrttis swam like locusts, clouding our discriminative faculty and reinforcing the faulty self-assessment that ignorance impresses on us. Nirodha is the means to regain the memory of who we truly are. We cease to identify with the vrttis. We realize that all of our turmoil, fears, doubts, anger, and depression are in the mind, not in the Self.

Patanjali taught many practices for stilling the mind so that we may end our misidentification with the activity of the vrttis and realize our true Self.

Now begins an explanation of Yoga.

Atha yoga anusasanam

"Anusasanam" means exposition or instruction, because it is not mere philosophy that Patanjali is about to expound, but rather direct instruction on how to practice Yoga. Mere philosophy will not satisfy us. We cannot achieve the goal by mere words alone. Without practice, nothing can be achieved.

Sri Swami Satchidananda

**Yoga is the cessation
of the misidentification with the
fluctuations of the mind.**
Yoga citta vrtti nirodhah

*The word "yoga" derives from the Sanskrit root "yuj"
meaning to unite, to join, to harness, to yoke, to contact,
or to connect . . . It is the union between the individual
self and the universal self . . . It is the joining of a healthy
body and a disciplined mind for spiritual development
. . . When the duality of matter and mind is totally
dissolved into the original source, the supreme goal of
yoga is achieved.*

Sri Swami Rajarshi Muni

Citta Vrtti

So you understand what is meant by citta. It is the mind-stuff, and vrttis are the waves and ripples rising in it when external causes impinge on it. These vrttis are our whole universe. The bottom of the lake we cannot see because its surface is covered with ripples. It is only possible when the ripples have subsided and the water is calm for us to catch a glimpse of the bottom. If the water is muddy, the bottom will not be seen; if the water is agitated all the time, the bottom will not be seen. If the water is clear and there are no waves, we shall see the bottom. That bottom of the lake is our own true Self: the lake is the citta, and the waves are the vrttis. Then, at last, when the waves cease and the water of the lake becomes clear, there is the state called sattva, serenity, and calmness. This citta is always trying to get back to its natural pure state, but the organs draw it out. To restrain it, and to check this outward tendency, and to start it on the return journey to that essence of intelligence is the first step in Yoga, because only in this way can the citta get into its proper course.

Sri Swami Vivekananda

Nirodha

As a lump of salt
thrown in water
dissolves
and cannot
be taken out again,
though wherever we taste the water
it is salty,
even so, beloved,
the separate self
dissolves
in the sea of pure
consciousness,
infinite and immortal.

Separateness arises from identifying
the Self with the body, which is
made up of the elements;
when this physical identification
dissolves there can be
no more separate self.

Brihadaranyaka Upanishad,
Chapter II, Verse 4.12

Then, the Seer dwells in its own true nature.

Tada drastuh svarupe vasthanam

This sutra points out in a general way what happens when all the modifications of the mind at all levels have been completely inhibited. The Seer is established in his Svarupa (i.e., form or truth) or in other words attains Self-realization. We cannot know what this state of Self-realization is as long as we are involved in the play of citta-vrttis.

Dr. I. K. Taimni

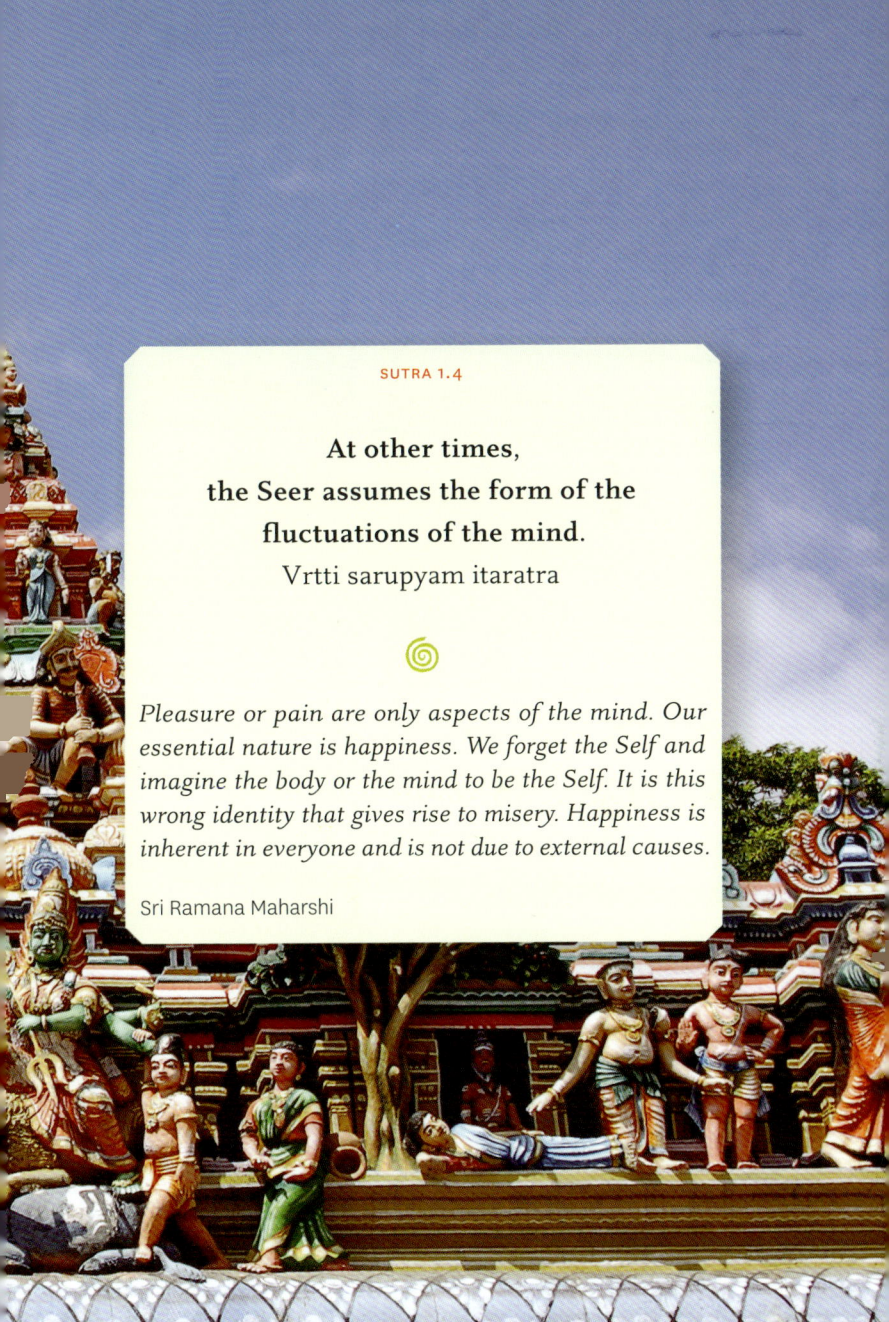

**At other times,
the Seer assumes the form of the
fluctuations of the mind.**

Vrtti sarupyam itaratra

*Pleasure or pain are only aspects of the mind. Our
essential nature is happiness. We forget the Self and
imagine the body or the mind to be the Self. It is this
wrong identity that gives rise to misery. Happiness is
inherent in everyone and is not due to external causes.*

Sri Ramana Maharshi

Vrttis: The Types of Mental Fluctuations

Oh, Krishna, the stillness of divine union
which you describe is beyond my comprehension.
How can the mind, which is so restless,
attain lasting peace?
Krishna, the mind is restless,
turbulent, powerful;
trying to control it is like trying to tame the wind.

Bhagavad Gita, Chapter 6, Verses 33–34

In Sutras 1.5-1.11, Patanjali describes the five types of vrttis: right knowledge, misconception, imagination, sleep, and memory. The vrttis in all of their varieties and combinations reflect the entire range of our mental activities. Since the goal of Yoga is to end our misidentification with the vrttis as stated in Sutra 1.2, the purpose of these sutras is to describe the vrttis so that we may recognize their affect on our minds and learn how to end their influence. As long as the vrttis are acting on the mind, the ego will identify with the vrttis, and the result will be a fragmented mind, a sense of alienation and obstruction in experiencing the true Self. This is the state referred to in Sutra 1.4.

The vrttis are like whirlpools that trap our minds in a vortex of con-stant mental activity. You can easily observe the vrttis if you attempt to enter into a few minutes of quiet awareness. As you begin to still and focus your mind on an object of meditation, you will notice a constant stream of imagery, thoughts, and associations, and you will have to consciously and constantly pull your attention back to the object of meditation. When I begin a meditation, I frequently notice an endless cacophony of mind noise such as office problems, the to do list, what I am having for dinner, and bodily sensations such as pain and numbness. My experience is always like trying to restrain the wind, as Arjuna laments in the passage from the Bhagavad Gita.

When we are held captive by the vrttis, we are constantly being tossed about like a boat on the rapids. We may regret the past, we may worry about the future, we may feel guilt over our actions or our failures, or we may feel many conflicting emotions and reactions from moment to moment as we interact with the world. We may become attached to the outcome of our activities and suffer if they do not meet our expectations. Because we experience and interact with the world through our ordinary minds, we are naturally drawn into identification with the vrtti activities and held captive. As long as we are subject to the vrittis, we are trapped in our individual egos, and access to our true Self is blocked. The entire practice of Yoga is aimed at breaking our misidentification with the vrttis so that the light and wisdom of the true Self can shine on our daily lives.

Some types of vrtti activity are helpful to us as we pursue our practice of Yoga. Patanjali classifies the vrttis into two broad categories: non-afflicted *(aklista)* and afflicted *(klista)*. Non-afflicted vrttis are those that arise through the practice of Yoga and facilitate the process of Self-realization. Non-afflicted vrttis are strengthened by practice and non-attachment, as we will more fully explore in Sutras 1.12–1.16. Importantly, the non-afflicted vrttis also dissolve the *klesas* and lead to the end of spiritual ignorance.

The klesas are often referred to as the afflictions, and as we will more fully explore in Pada Two, they are spiritual ignorance, ego, attachment, aversion, and clinging to bodily life. The klesas are the root cause of the vrttis. One of the keys to understanding the entire philosophy of the Yoga Sutras is that we must eliminate the klesas through Yoga practice to realize our true Self.

Afflicted vrttis are those vrttis that maintain the strength and influence of the klesas. In practicing Yoga, we dissolve our identification with the afflicted vrttis by strengthening the non-afflicted vrttis. As we attain higher states of spiritual knowledge, we can eventually release our identification with the non-afflicted vrttis as well.

Patanjali does not divide the vrttis into pleasurable and non-pleasurable categories. This is because even pleasurable thoughts and experiences can eventually lead to suffering. If you think of a great love in your life whom you have lost, you can easily see how something that once led to pleasurable thoughts can later lead to painful experiences of jealousy, unhappiness, and loss.

Ending our misidentification with the vrttis does not bring us pleasure. Rather, by ending the disturbances caused by the vrttis, we can realize our true Self and experience the joy and peace that were there all along.

There are five kinds of fluctuations. They are either aklista (non-afflictive) or klista (afflictive).

Vrttayah pancatayah klista aklistah

Patanjali says there are five kinds of vrittis, and again these are grouped into two major categories. One variety brings us pain; the other does not. Notice that he does not divide the thoughts into painful and pleasurable. Why? Because even a so-called pleasurable thought might ultimately bring us pain. And, again, we cannot easily know in the beginning whether a particular thought will bring pain or not. Some thoughts begin with pain but end leaving us at peace. Others appear to be pleasurable but bring pain.

Sri Swami Satchidananda

These five types of fluctuations
are right knowledge, misconception,
verbal delusion, deep sleep,
and memory.

Pramana viparyaya vikalpa nidra smrtayah

The sources of right knowledge are direct perception, inference, and spiritual texts and testimony.

Pratyaksa anumana agamah pramanani

Perception, inference, and verbal testimony are the three primary ways of right knowledge. How do we know that there is an object in front of us? We acquire this knowledge through direct sensory contact. This is perception. And when we see muddy water in a river, we suppose that there must have been rains uphill. This knowledge we gather by inference. The words of others in whom we have faith also convey to us true knowledge as, for example, when we believe that there is an elephant in the nearby city, on hearing of it from a reliable friend, though we might not have actually seen it with our eyes.

Sri Swami Krishnananda

Misconception is false knowledge that is not based upon the true form of an object.

Viparyayo mithya jnanam atad rupa pratistham

A coiled rope's speckled color and coiling are similar to those of a snake. And when the rope is perceived in a dim area, the thought arises, "This is a snake." As for the rope, at that time when it is seen to be a snake, the collection and parts of the rope are not even in the slightest way a snake. Therefore, that snake is merely set up by conceptuality.

H. H. Dalai Lama

Images arising from words that are not based on reality are fantasy.

Sabda jnana anupati vastu sunyo vikalpah

False imaginations rise from the consideration of appearances: things are discriminated as to form, signs, and shape; as to having color, warmth, humidity, motility or rigidity. False imagination consists in becoming attached to these appearances and their names. By reason of clinging to these false imaginations, there are multitudes of appearances which are imagined to be real but which are only imaginary.

The Lankavatara Sutra

Dreamless sleep is the state of mind without any content.

Abhava pratyaya alambana vrttir nidra

What is called "mind" is a wondrous power residing in the Self. It causes all thoughts to arise. Therefore, thought is the nature of mind. Apart from thoughts, there is no world. In deep sleep, there are no thoughts and there is no world. In the states of waking and dream, there are thoughts, and there is a world. Just as the spider emits the thread (of the web) out of itself and again withdraws it into itself, the mind projects the world out of itself and again resolves it into itself. When the mind comes out of the Self, the world appears. Therefore, when the world appears (to be real), the Self does not appear, and when the Self appears (shines), the world does not appear.

Sri Ramana Maharshi

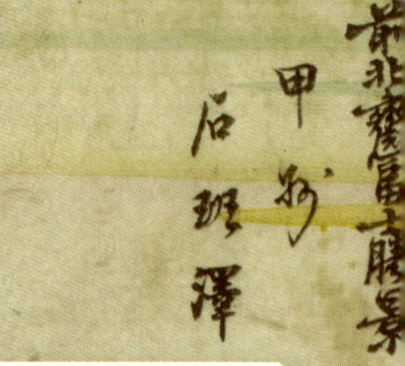

Memory is the direct recollection of a conscious experience.

Anubhuta visaya asampramosah smrtih

Memory is there. It contains our past conditioning: our childhood, our education, our culture (from which taste is molded), our experiences, our knowledge, our environment, our country, our family, our friends. Let us leave all this alone and not use those things, not exploit them or speculate upon them. They should remain there in a complete immobility like the background of a picture or a map. Not to carry them along is a blessing!

Vanda Scaravelli

Practice and Non-Attachment: Abhyasa and Vairagya

You have the right to work but never to the fruits of work. You should never engage in action for the sake of reward, nor should you long for inaction. Perform work in this world, Arjuna, as a man established within himself-without selfish attachments and alike in success and defeat. For yoga is perfect evenness of mind. Seek refuge in the attitude of detachment, and you will amass the wealth of spiritual awareness. Those who are motivated only by desire for the fruits of action are miserable, for they are constantly anxious about the results of what they do. When consciousness is unified, however, all vain anxiety is left behind. There is no cause for worry, whether things go well or ill. Therefore, devote yourself to the disciplines of yoga, for yoga is skill in action.

Bhagavad Gita, Chapter 2, Verses 47–50

Patanjali taught that the path to eliminating the fluctuations of our minds (i.e., the vrttis) is through consistent, devoted practice (*abhyasa*) and detachment from the results of that practice *(vairagya)*. B. K. S. Iyengar observes: "Practice is the positive aspect of Yoga; detachment or renunciation (vairagya) the negative. The two balance each other like day and night, inhalation and exhalation." These principles are the two poles of our Yoga practice.

Patanjali takes an open and inclusive approach to Yoga practice and describes over twenty separate practices within the Yoga Sutras. These include devotional practices, meditations, mantras, pranayama, Kriya Yoga, and Astanga Yoga (described in Sutras 2.1 and 2.29, respectively). Achieving the proper balance between a dedicated and successful practice and non-attachment to the results of that practice may be difficult because we often view these goals as paradoxical. This paradox is aggravated in Western cultures because we tend to be achievement and goal oriented.

Sri Swami Satchidananda observes that vairagya (non-attachment) literally means colorless or without color. Each desire brings its own unique color into the mind. A mind that is colored with selfish motives becomes restless, and practice suffers as a result. Colored desires are like ripples in our minds that create restlessness and distraction and obstruct our practice. However, desires that are not driven by selfishness, such as the desire to serve others, do not color the mind.

Non-attachment is fundamentally an exercise in discrimination. We must carefully examine the goal or object we are considering by asking ourselves: Why do I really want this object? Am I motivated by my ego, or am I motivated by the wisdom of my heart? Will reaching this goal lead me closer to a state of greater Yogic wisdom or will it lead me down a path of suffering? When we are thinking about setting goals, we need to carefully discern the motivation of the goal.

It is quite easy to set a goal without looking deeply into the motivation behind the goal or the results that will flow from attaining the goal. Ultimately we must decide if the goal is the result of ego, desire, and restlessness of the mind or is it driven by something that will lead us more deeply into Yoga?

The twin principles of practice and non-attachment arise during my Yoga practice. If I allow myself to become attached to my desire to progress up the asana ladder, I may become ego-centered and begin competing with the other students in the class. This causes me to lose awareness of my body, and I forget to breathe. I tighten my muscles, and I fall out of the pose. This, in turn, triggers a mental cycle of self-criticism and judgment, which pulls me even further from the present moment. The attachment to a goal disrupts the flow of my practice.

Attachment acts as a trigger for my ego to become involved in my practice. When my ego becomes involved, my consciousness becomes constricted and narrow. I may get wrapped up in my personal stories, my desire to achieve and excel, and my anxieties and disappointments when I do not get what I want. This is the opposite of the state of Yoga I should be practicing to attain: a state in which my mind is centered in the present and is open and expansive.

On the other hand, if I focus too much on non-attachment, I may become apathetic, non-attentive, and begin to daydream. I may not push my poses to their edge or maintain my concentration. An attitude of non-attachment gives me an excuse to avoid challenging poses and practicing with the intensity that will expand my practice. Again, the result is that I do not reap the full benefit of the practice.

However, if I can keep both principles firmly in mind and in balance through constant awareness, my practice becomes deeper. One way to think of these two principles is to imagine that they are the two wings of a bird. Both are needed for the bird to fly.

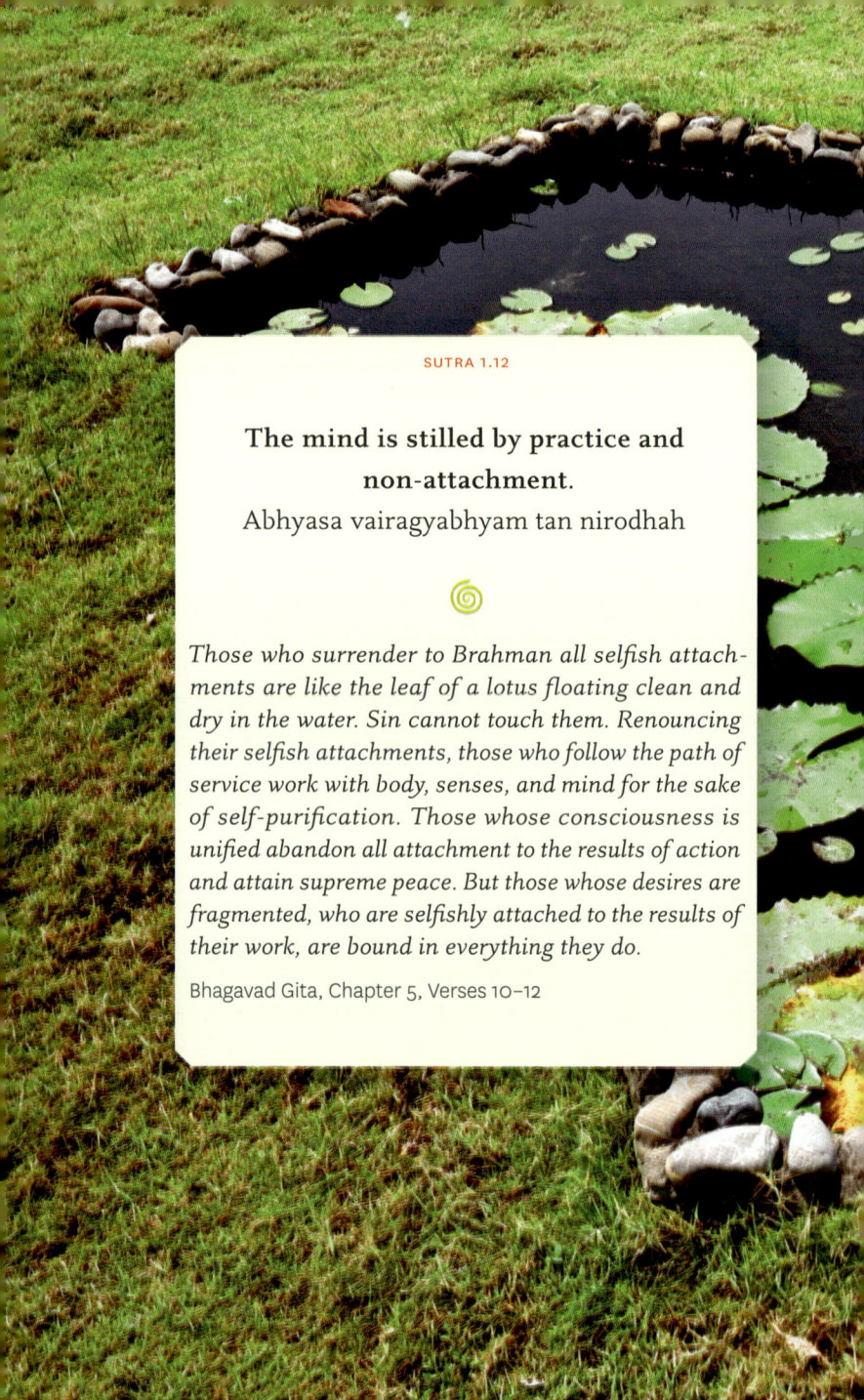

The mind is stilled by practice and non-attachment.

Abhyasa vairagyabhyam tan nirodhah

Those who surrender to Brahman all selfish attachments are like the leaf of a lotus floating clean and dry in the water. Sin cannot touch them. Renouncing their selfish attachments, those who follow the path of service work with body, senses, and mind for the sake of self-purification. Those whose consciousness is unified abandon all attachment to the results of action and attain supreme peace. But those whose desires are fragmented, who are selfishly attached to the results of their work, are bound in everything they do.

Bhagavad Gita, Chapter 5, Verses 10–12

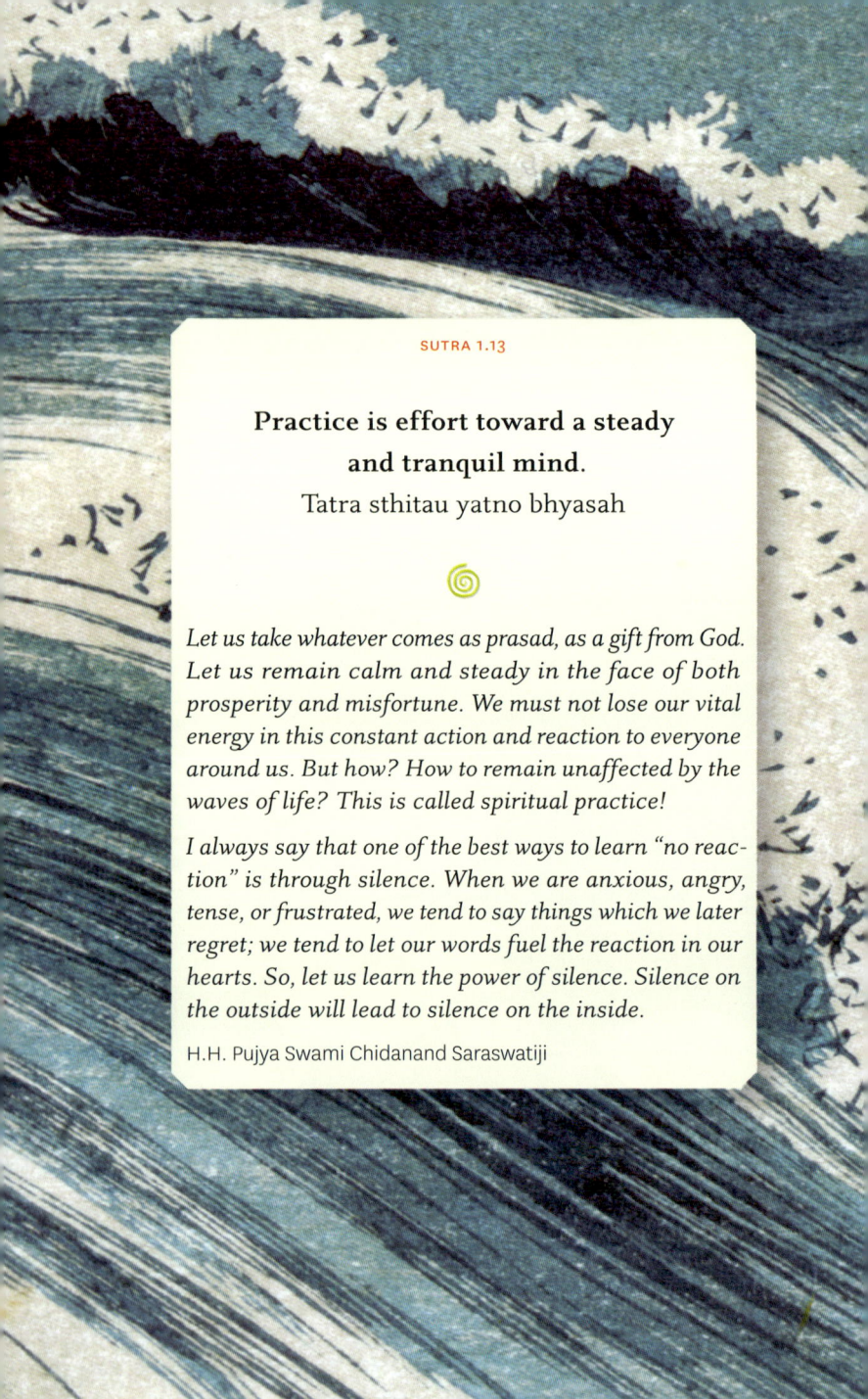

Practice is effort toward a steady and tranquil mind.

Tatra sthitau yatno bhyasah

Let us take whatever comes as prasad, as a gift from God. Let us remain calm and steady in the face of both prosperity and misfortune. We must not lose our vital energy in this constant action and reaction to everyone around us. But how? How to remain unaffected by the waves of life? This is called spiritual practice!

I always say that one of the best ways to learn "no reaction" is through silence. When we are anxious, angry, tense, or frustrated, we tend to say things which we later regret; we tend to let our words fuel the reaction in our hearts. So, let us learn the power of silence. Silence on the outside will lead to silence on the inside.

H.H. Pujya Swami Chidanand Saraswatiji

Practice becomes firmly grounded when continued for a long time with devotion and right action.

Sa tu dirgha kala nairantarya satkara asevito drdha bhumih

There is the practice of Yoga
Of the body, mind and atma (i.e., spirit)—
Always fruitful, and it gives to each
through practice what he seeks.
Follow the teachings of the guru.
Meditate on the feet of the Lord.
Practice faithfully astanga yoga.
Realize joy or mukti as you choose.

T. Krishnamacharya, Verses 12- 13

**Non-attachment (vairagya)
is freedom from craving for objects that
are seen or described in scriptures.**
Drsta anusravika visaya vitrsnasya
vasikara samjña vairagyam

*Mahamati, the ignorant, not knowing that the world is
only something seen of the mind itself, cling to external
objects, to the notions of being and non-being, oneness
and otherness, existence and non-existence, and think
that they have a self-nature of their own, all of which
rises from the discriminations of the mind.*

*It is like the city of the Gandharvas, which the unwitting
take to be a real city though it is not so in fact. The city
appears as in a vision owing to their attachment to the
memory of a city preserved in the mind as a seed; the
city can thus be said to be both existent and non-existent.*

The Lankavatara Sutra

**The highest kind of non-attachment is
when one transcends the qualities
of nature (the gunas) and perceives the
true Self (Purusha).**

Tat param purusa khyater guna vaitrsnyam

Monks sit peacefully among the trees,
ridding themselves of illusion with a calm mind.
Quietly realizing enlightenment,
they experience a joy that is beyond that of heaven.
Laymen seek fame and profit,
of fine robes, seats, and bedding.
Though the joy in getting them is only fleeting,
they are untiring in their quest.

Monks, however, beg for food in humble robes,
their daily actions being one with the Way.
With their Wisdom-eye opened
they realize the essence of the Law.

Zen Master Dogen

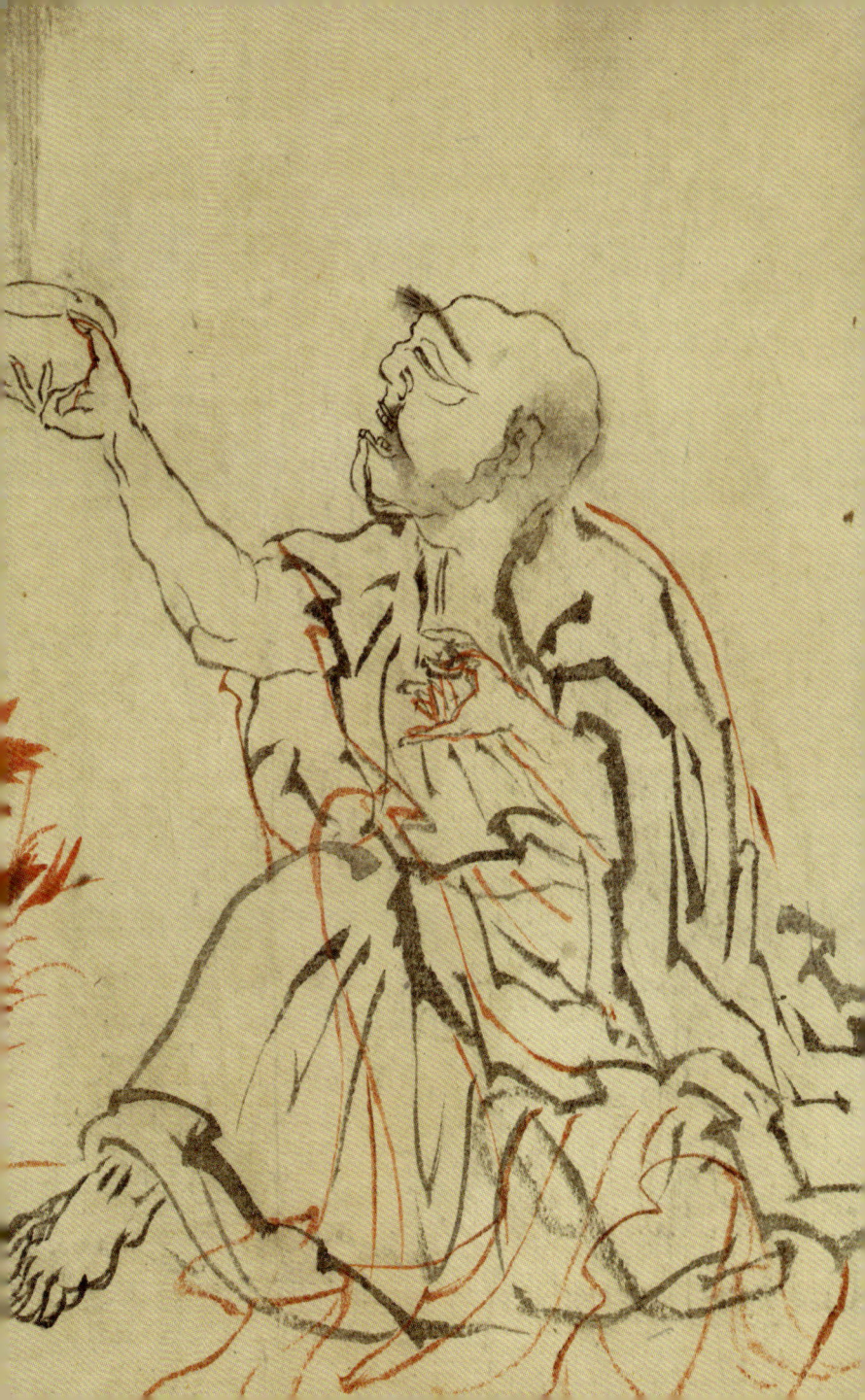

Samadhi: The Two Stages

As salt dissolves in water, so the mind dissolves into the soul and becomes one with it. The unity of soul and mind is called samadhi.

Hatha Yoga Pradipika

Samadhi is perfect concentration, which is the goal of the Yogi.

Sri Swami Vivekananda

Samadhi is one of the most complex and important topics in the Yoga Sutras and is a key to understanding Yoga philosophy and practice. Samadhi is often translated as contemplation, absorption, or concentration. It is the process of penetrating into deeper and deeper layers of consciousness with the goal of reaching the true Self. As we will learn when we encounter Astanga Yoga in Sutra 2.29, samadhi is the last of the eight limbs of Yoga, and it is the goal of our Yoga practice.

This inner journey occurs through the many practices described by Patanjali. For beginning practitioners, the goal is to achieve a pure, calm, and stable mind so that they can taste the state of samadhi. For more advanced practitioners who already have calm minds, these practices enable them to experience deeper and deeper stages of samadhi.

SAMPRAJNATA SAMADHI

Patanjali describes two kinds of samadhi: samprajnata and asamprajnata. In *samprajnata samadhi*, the mind focuses on an object that is used as a prop. The object could be a candle, a flower, a religious icon, a deity, or any other object with special meaning. As the mind concentrates and becomes absorbed in the object, consciousness is drawn from its center outward toward the object. The mind begins to become identified and united with the object. Samprajnata samadhi describes a range of experiences as this unity becomes more and more complete. In samadhi we experience deeper and deeper states of awareness until we realize the true Self.

There are four stages of samprajnata samadhi. We begin our journey by contemplating physical objects. We progress by contemplating more and more subtle objects and then states of awareness until we reach the blissful state. By contemplating and becoming absorbed in these objects and states, we become united with them. We leave our everyday minds behind and gain a new form of knowledge.

This knowledge is not based on intellectual, logical analysis or the scientific method. Rather, it is direct and intuitive knowledge that arises by achieving a state of unity with the object being contemplated. As the normal distinction between ourselves as the subject and the outside world as an object dissolves, we begin to experience the true Self. This is yogic knowledge.

The four stages of samprajnata samadhi are: (1) *vitarka* (gross objects), (2) *vicara* (more subtle objects), (3) *ananda* (the state of joy and bliss), and (4) *asmita* (the state of only the "I"). Sri Swami Satchidananda describes these stages as follows:

Patanjali further divides the samprajnata samadhi into four forms. To understand them, we have to understand the makeup of what he calls nature, or Prakriti. According to Patanjali, Prakriti also has four divisions: the very gross material; the subtle elements, which ultimately express as the concrete forms which you see; the mind-stuff; and the ego or the individuality. So, samadhi is practiced first on the gross objects (savitarka samadhi), then on to the subtle elements (savichara samadhi), then on the mind devoid of any objects except its own joy—in other words the sattvic mind (sa-ananda samadhi)— and then finally on the "I" feeling alone (sa-asmita samadhi). There is a gradation because you can't immediately contemplate the very subtle.

I like to mediate upon my wooden statue of Ganesha, which I bought in India. He is quite old and is painted in faded ochre, orange, and red colors.

In the first stage of samprajnata samadhi (i.e., vitarka), I concentrate upon the statue and become intensely aware of its many fine details: the ornamentation in the crown, the design of the sweet in the outstretched hand, the flowing orange of the drapes, the beautiful cracked blue of the goad, the roundness of the mala beads, the sweep of the elephant ears, and the purple mouse. I begin to experience a sense that my everyday mind has fallen away, and its thought processes have slowed down or stopped altogether. The only thing that exists in the world is Ganesha.

As my experience of the image becomes more and more vivid and subtle details of the statute become revealed, I begin to feel a resonance with the qualities that Ganesha represents, such as Lord of Obstacles, or his association with OM. This is the second stage of samprajnata samadhi (i.e., vicara).

As I relax and move more deeply into the experience, my everyday mind falls away, cares and worries fade, and I begin to feel relaxed and joyful. I have entered the third stage of samprajnata samadhi (i.e., ananda).

The final stage is asmita, and it is described by Sri Swami Krishnananda as follows:

In this asmita state, the world ceases to be an external atmosphere or an environment that is outside us. It becomes an emanating force of our own personality. We do not live in a world anymore; we live in our own Self. We do not walk on the streets; we enjoy the bliss of our infinity, and the things of the world cease to be things inanimate. The inanimate character of the objects ceases. It is not matter that we are looking at, but vital force—energy that is living, as much alive as the living consciousness which is experiencing this.

ASAMPRAJNATA SAMADHI

In *asamprajnata samadhi* there is no object that is used to focus the mind. Rather, consciousness is focused solely on the true Self. The ego is transcended, and the mind is perfectly still. There is no subject, and there is no object. The conscious mind is completely still, and no thoughts ripple through the mind. This is a very high state of awareness in which there is unity with the true Self.

In the Yoga Sutras, Patanjali established three primary systems of Yoga. The first is described within the Samadhi Pada, which is the first chapter of the Yoga Sutras. This system is for advanced practitioners who have already attained a state of mental calm and purity. For these yogis, practice involves a variety of techniques such as breath control, concentration on enlightened beings or the blissful inner light, or meditating on spiritually uplifting objects.

The other two systems are in the second chapter of the Yoga Sutras, which is known as the Sadhana Pada. *Sadhana* is a Sanskrit word that means "dedicated practice." This chapter was written for beginning practitioners to enable them to develop a pure and stable mind so that they can begin the more advanced practices that will lead to samadhi. In the Sadhana Pada, Patanjali established the systems of Kriya Yoga and Astanga Yoga.

Kriya Yoga involves discipline (*tapas*), the study of spiritual books (*svadhyaya*), and surrender to the Supreme Being (*Isvara pranidhanani*). It is described in Sutra 2.1.

Astanga Yoga is known as the eight-limbed path and is comprised of *yama* (the restraints), *niyama* (the observances), *asana* (posture), *pranayama* (breath control), *pratyahara* (sense-withdrawal), *dharana* (concentration), *dhyana* (meditation), and *samadhi* (absorption). It is established in Sutra 2.29.

The states of samprajnata and asamprajnata samadhi are extremely refined and subtle states of consciousness that may be reached only after years of dedicated practice under the guidance of a teacher. These states go beyond the intellectual knowledge that is gained through our intellect, our senses, or our study of books. Ultimately, samadhi is knowledge of the true Self. This experience is beyond our ability to describe in words, but the writings of such mystics as Sri Aurobindo, Ramana Maharshi, Ramakrishna, Rumi, Meister Eckhart, and Saint Theresa of Avila point the way to the experience. However, as we will see in Sutra 1.19, some practitioners, rather than reaching their true Self, falsely identify with the natural world and lose their way.

**Samprajnata samadhi is
reached through concentration on gross
objects, subtle objects, blissfulness, and
pure I-am-ness.**

Vitarka vicara ananda asmita rupa
anugamat samprajnatah

*Patanjali saw in the evolving process of meditation
several broad but distinct levels of samadhi. The first
is samprajnata samadhi, cognitive contemplation, in
which the meditator is aware of a distinction between
himself and the thought he entertains. This form of
meditation is also called sabija samadhi, or meditation with a seed (bija), wherein some object or specific
theme serves as a focal point on which to settle the
mind in a steady state. Since such a point is extrinsic
to pure consciousness, the basic distinction between
thinker and thought persists. In its least abstracted
form, samprajnata samadhi involves vitarka (reason-
ing), vicara (deliberation), ananda (bliss), and asmita
(the sense of "I").*

Raghavan Iyer

Asamprajnata samadhi is the cessation of mental fluctuations so that only latent impressions remain.

Virama pratyaya abhyasa purvah samskara sesa anyah

In samprajnata samadhi, the buried seeds can still come into the conscious mind when the proper opportunity is given and pull you into worldly experience. That is why all of these four stages should be passed, and you should get into asamprajnata samadhi, where even the ego feeling is not there and the seeds of past impressions are rendered harmless. In that state, only the conscious-ness is there and nothing else. Once that is achieved, the individual is completely liberated, and there is no more coming into the world and getting tossed.

Sri Swami Satchidananda

Some advanced yogis who are merged
into nature (Prakriti) or
who are bodiless are reborn
(and lose the path to liberation).
Bhava pratyayo videha
prakriti layanam

Concentration without non-attachment cannot bring liberation. However hard we may struggle, we can only be rewarded in accordance with our desires. If we really want liberation and work hard enough for it, we shall get it. But if we really want power and pleasure, we can get them instead—not only in this world and in this human form but in other worlds and other forms hereafter.

Christopher Isherwood

The Quality of Practice

There are three kinds of dolls: the first made of salt, the second made of cloth, and the third made of stone. If these dolls be immersed in water, the first will get dissolved and lose its form, the second will absorb a large quantity of water but retain its form, while the third will be impervious to the water. The first doll represents the man who merges his self in the Universal and All-pervading Self and becomes one with it, that is the "Mukta Purusha." The second represents a true lover, or Bhakta, who is full of Divine bliss and knowledge; and the third represents a worldly man who will not absorb the least drop of true knowledge.

Sri Ramakrishna

One who depends on fate or destiny and doesn't make an effort remains sitting-like one who sits by the seashore waiting for a pearl to wash up.

Baba Hari Dass

In these sutras, Patanjali describes the qualities of practice that are necessary to progress along the path of Yoga. These are faith, strength, mindfulness, meditation, and wisdom.

Faith is the firm conviction that the practice of Yoga will enable us to reach our true Self. It is an inner certainty that the practice of Yoga is a true path. Without faith in the path, how can we sustain the long, difficult and dedicated practice that Yoga requires? We also need faith in our teachers and faith in ourselves to continue our practice even when it becomes hard. Strength gives us the determination and courage necessary to overcome the doubts, distractions, and other obstacles that the modern world seems to place in our way. Through mindfulness, the third quality, we can understand the mistakes that we have made and learn from them so that we may progress, rather than repeating them again and again. Finally, meditation leads to the discriminative wisdom that we need to attain the highest states of Yoga.

These sutras explain how differences in the quality of our practice lead to different results. If we practice with intensity, vigor, and conviction, we will achieve the fruits of Yoga more quickly than if we practice only occasionally. Is our practice disconnected from our everyday lives, or does it infuse our lives and actions with its insights and wisdom? Do we leave our Yoga on the mat, or do we take it out into the world? Can we use our Yogic wisdom to navigate conflicts at the office, economic pressures, and family difficulties? Can we inspire positive change in ourselves and in others? These are some questions to consider if we want an intense and dedicated practice that will help us progress more rapidly in our Yoga practice.

For others, the path is faith, energy, mindfulness, meditation, and wisdom.

Sraddha virya smrti samadhi prajña
purvaka itaresam

The practice of meditation frees one from all affliction. This is the path of Yoga. Follow it with determination and sustained enthusiasm. Renouncing wholeheartedly all selfish desires and expectations, use your will to control the senses. Little by little, through patience and repeated effort, the mind will become stilled in the Self.

The Bhagavad Gita, Chapter 6, Verses 23–25

It is near for those whose practice is intense.

Tivra samveganam asannah

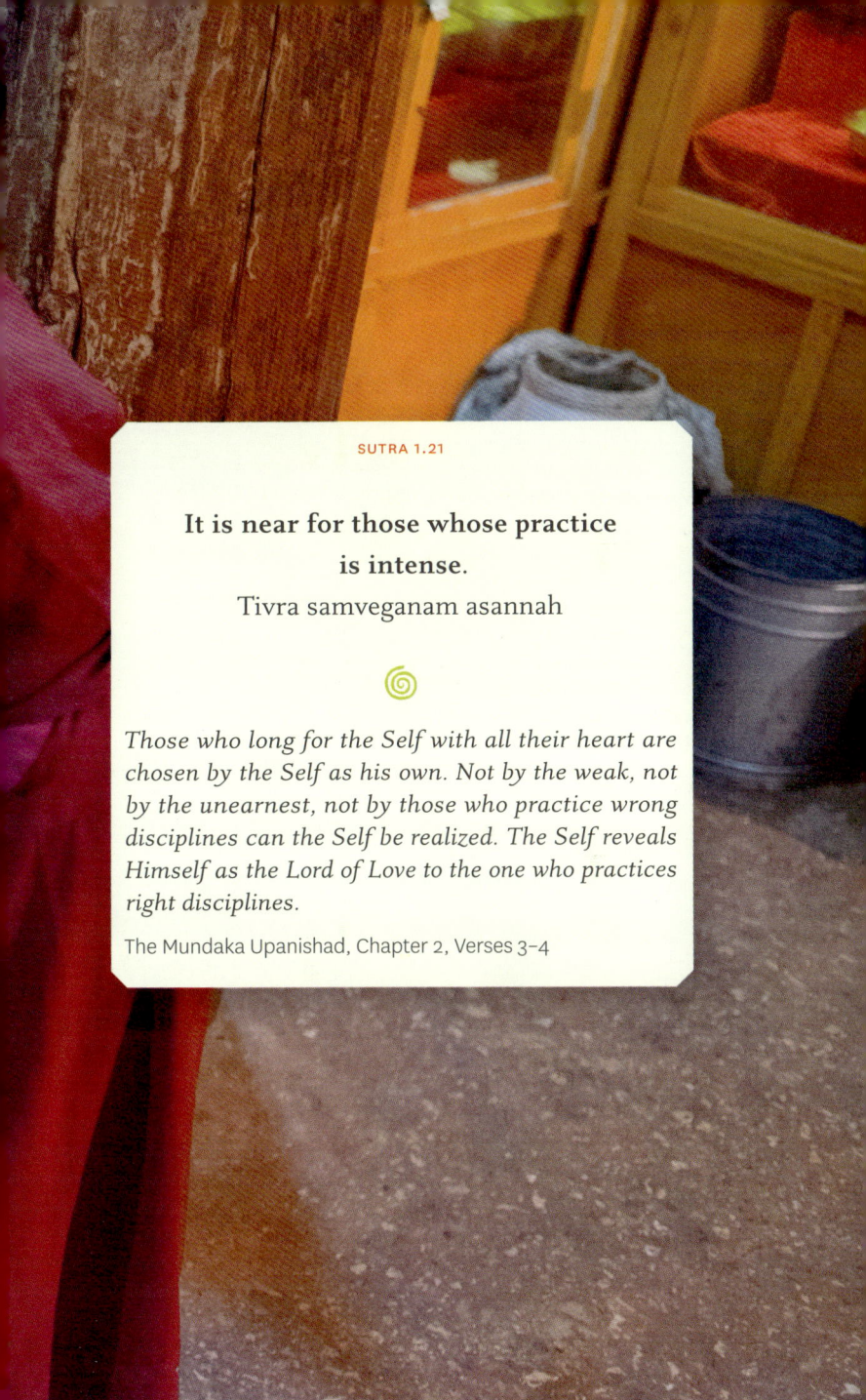

Those who long for the Self with all their heart are chosen by the Self as his own. Not by the weak, not by the unearnest, not by those who practice wrong disciplines can the Self be realized. The Self reveals Himself as the Lord of Love to the one who practices right disciplines.

The Mundaka Upanishad, Chapter 2, Verses 3–4

There are differences among those whose practice is mild, moderate, or intense.

Mrdu madhya adhimatratvat tatah
api visesah

A person is what his deep desire is. It is our deepest desire in this life that shapes the life to come. So let us direct our deepest desires to realize the Self.

The Chandogya Upanishad, Chapter 3, Verse 14.1

Isvara and Mantra

With every breath I plant the seeds of devotion—
I am a farmer of the heart.
Day and night I see the face of union—
I am the mirror of God.
Every moment I shape the destiny with a chisel—
I am a carpenter of my own soul.

Rumi

All things are created by the Om;
The love-form is His body.
He is without form, without quality,
without decay:
Seek thou union with Him!
But that formless God takes a thousand forms
in the eyes of His creatures:
He is pure and indestructible,
His form is infinite and fathomless,
He dances in rapture,
and waves of form arise from His dance.
The body and the mind
cannot contain themselves
when they are touched by His great joy.
He is immersed in all consciousness,
all joys, and all sorrows;
He has no beginning and no end;
He holds all within His bliss.

Kabir

In Sutra 1.23, Patanjali provides us with yet another path to Self-realization: the practice of *Isvara pranidhanani*. This is usually translated as devotion or surrender to the Supreme Being. It is a practice that is at the core of the bhakti spiritual path. Sri Swami Satchidananda beautifully describes this practice:

It is surrendering to the Supreme Being, I understand this to mean dedicating the fruits of your actions to God or to humanity—god in manifestation. Dedicate everything—your study, your japa [recitation of a mantra], your practices—to the Lord. When you give such things to Him, He accepts them but then gives them back many times magnified. Even virtuous, meritorious deeds will bind you in some form if you do them with an egoistic feeling. Every time you do something, feel, "May this be dedicated to the Lord." If you constantly remember to do this, the mind will be free and tranquil.

In this block of sutras, Patanjali sheds light on the nature of Isvara. *Isvara* is the Supreme Being who has never been touched by avidya (ignorance), karma, or the activities of nature (i.e., Prakriti). For this reason, Isvara possesses the extraordinary ability of knowing and understanding everything. This is the basis for Sutra 1.26, which states that Isvara is the great teacher, or first guru, of the sages since the beginning of time.

Patanjali draws a subtle distinction between Isvara and Purusha. As more fully discussed in connection with Sutras 2.17–2.24, Purusha is the true Self. Isvara is an extraordinary Purusha, separate and apart from the "ordinary" Purusha. Isvara is the Supreme Being in any form that we may conceive of such a Being within our personal tradition. Isvara is the object of our devotional practices.

In Sutra 1.28, Patanjali said that we should chant "OM" and meditate on its meaning. This is the practice of mantra. A mantra is a series of sacred sounds that have the inherent power to change consciousness through the vibrations caused by the sounds. Mantra may be the most common and

powerful of all meditation practices.

The Sanskrit word *mantra* has two parts: *man* which is the root of the word for mind, and *tra* which is the root of the word for instrument. Chanting a mantra has the power to lift our awareness from our ordinary minds to deeper levels of awareness. It can liberate us from the suffering caused by our identification with our everyday, egoic minds. Mantras can help us with improving our concentration, being more patient at work, with our sense of well-being, and in dealing with negative thoughts and emotions.

There are many types of mantras. Some are longer prayers such as the Gayatri mantra. The Gayatri mantra is a prayer to Surya, the Vedic God of the Sun. Other mantras are the divine names of deities, such as OM Nama Shivaya for Lord Shiva. Practitioners of bhakti Yoga use mantra to identify with the divine.

Other forms of mantra are *bija*, or seed mantras. These are very powerful single syllables. They may represent goddesses, the elements or the chakras. Examples of seed mantras are sounds such as: *lam*, *vam*, *ram*, and *yam*.

OM is the most important mantra. Om is the sacred sound. OM is the ground of all being without beginning or end. OM is the creative vibration from divine consciousness that manifests spirit into all forms of matter. By chanting OM, our bodies and minds resonate with the energy of the universe, and our consciousness is transformed.

Samadhi is also attained by devotion to Isvara.

Isvara pranidhanad va

Here he (Patanjali) says that there is another way to get success: Isvara pranidhanam, or self-surrender to God. By the term Isvara, Patanjali means the supreme consciousness—not the individual soul but the supreme soul.

Sri Swami Satchidananda

**Isvara is a special Purusha.
He is untouched by afflictions (klesas),
actions (karma), and their results.**
Klesa karma vipaka asayair aparamrstah
purusa visesa isvarah

*What is Isvara? First of all it is a name, a concept that,
as I have said, describes the highest divine being. Isvara
does not belong to the material world (prakrti), or to the
seer in us (purusha). Isvara is distinguished by these
qualities: Isvara sees all things as they are; his action
is perfect; he is omniscient, the first teacher, a source
of help and support. Unlike us, Isvara is not subject
to the influence of avidya. Although he is acquainted
with avidya, he remains untouched by it.*

T. K. V. Desikachar

Isvara is the unsurpassed seed of all knowledge.

Tatra niratisayam sarva jña bijam

In this world, there are two orders of being: the perishable, separate creature and the changeless spirit. But beyond these there is another, the supreme Self, the eternal Lord, who enters into the entire cosmos and supports it from within.

I am that supreme Self, praised by the scriptures as beyond the changing and the changeless. Those who see in me that supreme Self see truly. They have found the source of all wisdom, Arjuna, and they worship me with all their heart.

Bhagavad Gita, Chapter 15, Verses 16–19

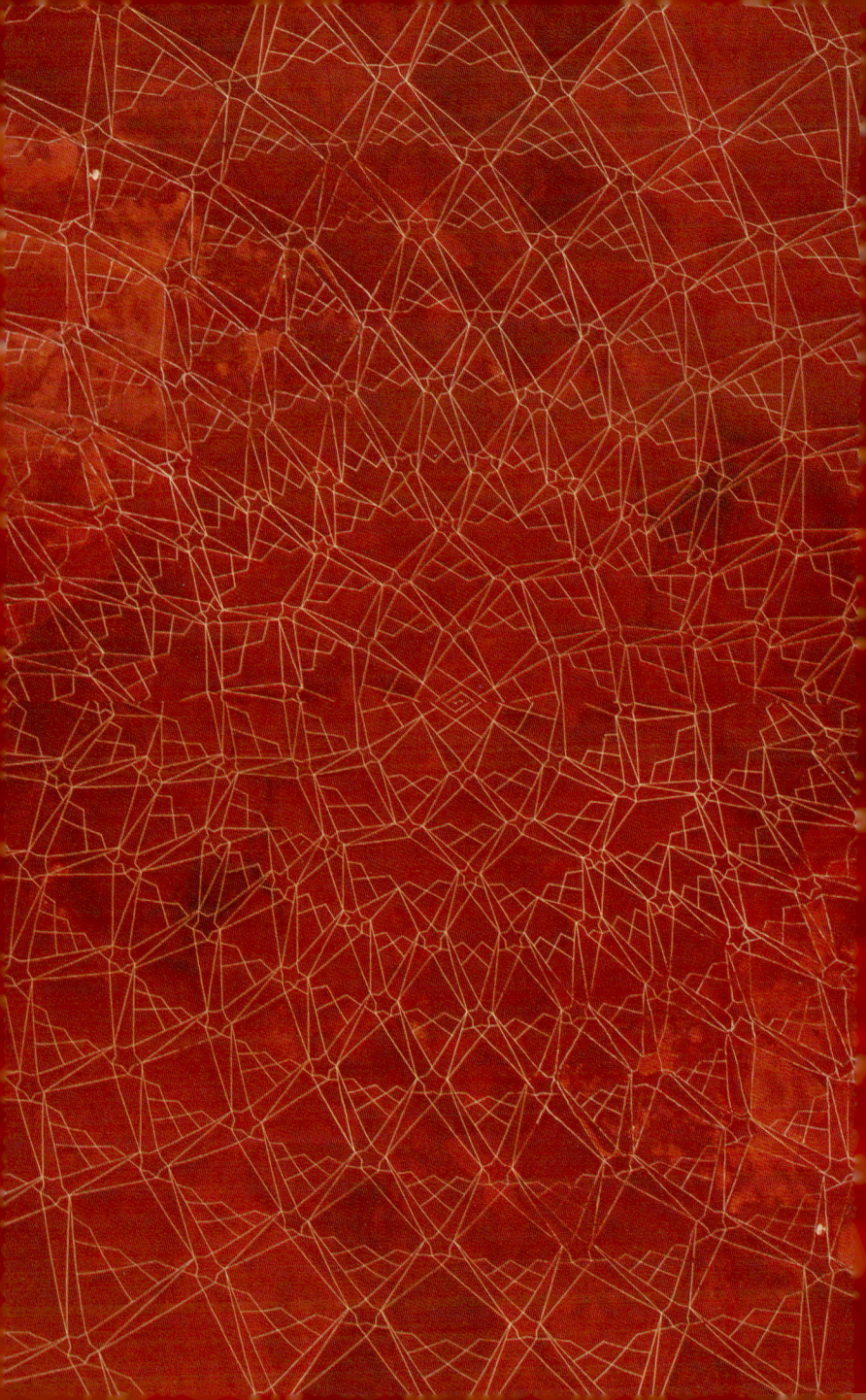

Isvara is the guru of the ancient teachers from beginningless time.

Purvesam api guruh kalena anavacchedat

O brother, my heart yearns for that true Guru,
who fills the cup of true love,
and drinks of it himself,
and offers it then to me.
He removes the veil from the eyes,
and gives the true vision of Brahma.
He reveals the worlds in Him,
and makes me to hear the Unstruck Music.
He shows joy and sorrow to be one.
He fills all utterance with love.
Verily he has no fear,
who has such a Guru
to lead him to the shelter of safety.

Kabir

The sacred word representing Isvara is pranava (OM).

Tasya vacakah pranavah

I sat alone on a block of stone
On the banks of the Ganges.
Mother Ganges blessed me.

I meditated on OM
and its meaning–
The Word that is the symbol of Brahman.

The little personality was lost.
The mortal limit of the self was loosened.

But there was infinite extension.
I entered into the Nameless beyond;
I realized the quintessential unity of bliss.

Sri Swami Sivananda

**Let there be the chanting
of that (OM) with meditation
on its meaning.**

Taj japas tad artha bhavanam

OM

*In each of the three planes of existence
We collect ourselves and meditate upon
That wonderous Spirit of the divine Solar Being.
We pray for the divine light to illuminate our minds.*

OM

*Bhur bhuvah svah
Tat savitur varenyam
Bhargo devasya dhimahi
Dhiyo yo nah pracodayat*

The Rig Veda (3:62:10)

The Obstacles to Calming the Mind

Pleasure, pain, love, hate, anger, fear are born with the mind and are fed by the mind. They exist as long as the mind exists. When pure consciousness dawns, the mind with its products disappears.

Baba Hari Dass

All that we are is the result of what we have thought: it is founded on our thoughts; it is made up of our thoughts. If a man speaks or acts with an evil thought, pain follows him, as the wheel follows the foot of the ox that draws the carriage. All that we are is the result of what we have thought: it is founded on our thoughts; it is made up of our thoughts.

If a man speaks or acts with a pure thought, happiness follows him, like a shadow that never leaves him. "He abused me, he beat me, he defeated me, he robbed me." In those who harbor such thoughts hatred will never cease. "He abused me, he beat me, he defeated me, he robbed me." In those who do not harbor such thoughts, hatred will cease. For hatred does not cease by hatred at any time: hatred ceases by love—this is an old rule.

Lord Buddha, The Dhammapada: "The Twin Verses"

These sutras describe the obstacles that prevent progress on the spiritual path. These obstacles block our practice because they make it difficult for us to calm our minds. The obstacles are divided into physical, mental, intellectual, and spiritual categories. They create sorrow, depression, despair, agitation, and irregular breathing.

For example, sometimes I bring my daily problems into a Yoga class and obsess over what I should have said or done in the situation that is troubling me. Because I am stuck in the past, I cannot center in the present moment. This makes it difficult for me to experience my poses fully. My breathing becomes erratic and forced, my poses fall apart, and I become disappointed in the quality of my practice. This disappointment creates more mental disturbances, and my practice degrades even more. The inevitable result is, as Patanjali said, "instability in the yogic state." However, when I begin class with a calm and present mind, my breathing relaxes and flows, the poses build naturally and comfortably, and my practice becomes centered, serene, and beneficial.

Patanjali taught that commitment to a single truth or principle, known as *abhyasa*, helps us to overcome the obstacles. We are free to decide which truth or principle we wish to follow. For example, Mahatma Ghandi dedicated his life to the principle of *satyagraha* (insistence on truth) both as a spiritual practice and as a way to liberate India from British rule. A contemporary example of abhyasa might be to practice the principle of non-violence (*ahimsa*) by adopting a vegetarian diet. Because ahimsa is the first yama of the eight limbs of Yoga, it has special importance in the practice of Yoga. Without non-violence, we have no Yoga practice.

We can keep our minds calm by cultivating a positive attitude toward all beings. In Sutra 1.33, Patanjali provided us with guidance on inter- acting with other people. Perhaps he did this because interacting with

other people in a positive way is one of the most difficult things we do.

Patanjali placed people in one of four personality types: happy, unhappy, virtuous, and wicked. We should be friendly toward the happy, compassionate toward the unhappy, delightful toward the virtuous, and calm toward the wicked.

Sri Swami Satchidananda refers to Sutra 1.33 as the four locks and the four keys. He observes:

Who would not like serenity of mind always? Who would not like to be happy always? Everybody wants that. So Patanjali gives four keys: friendliness, compassion, delight and disregard. There are only four kinds of locks in the world. Keep these four keys always with you, and when you come across any one of these four locks, you will have the proper key to open it. What are these four locks? Sukha, duhka, punya, and apunya—the happy people, the unhappy people, the virtuous, and the wicked. At any given moment, you can fit any person into one of these four categories.

From this practice (meditation on OM),
obstacles disappear, and the true Self is
realized.

Tatah pratyakcetana adhigamah api antaraya
abhavah ca

One of the basic mantras is, of course, the word spelled
OM. That sound is used because it contains the whole
range of the voice and it represents the total energy of
the universe. This word is called the pravana, the name
for the Ultimate Reality. And so in this way, if you chant
it, and vary it, and keep it up for quite a long time, you
find that the words will become pure sound. You will
become completely absorbed in the sound and find
yourself living in an eternal now in which there is no
past and there is no future, and there is no difference
between you as knower and what you are as the known,
between yourself and the world of nature outside you.

Alan Watts

The obstacles that distract the mind are disease, idleness, doubt, carelessness, laziness, sensuality, delusion, spiritual failure, and instability in the yogic state.

Vyadhi styana samsaya pramada alasya avirati bhranti darsana alabdha bhumikatva anavasthitatvani citta viksepas te antarayah

It is good to tame the mind, which is difficult to hold in and flighty, rushing wherever it listeth; a tamed mind brings happiness. Let the wise man guard his thoughts, for they are difficult to perceive, very artful, and they rush wherever they list: thoughts well guarded bring happiness.

Lord Buddha, The Dhammapada: "Thought"

**These obstacles are accompanied
with sorrow, despair,
restlessness of the body, and
irregular breathing.**
Duhkha daurmanasya angam ejayatva
svasa prasvasa viksepa sahabhuvah

*A sickly body can never be fit to sit; it will not allow the
mind to meditate quietly. Weak nerves will always create tremors. When some people meditate, they tremble
and perspire. These are symptoms of physical weakness.
But such things will not happen if we keep our body
in proper condition by right diet, exercise, proper rest
and if we do not allow it to be lazy or dull.*

Sri Swami Satchidananda

The practice of concentrating on a single principle prevents the obstacles.

Tat pratisedha artham eka
tattva abhyasah

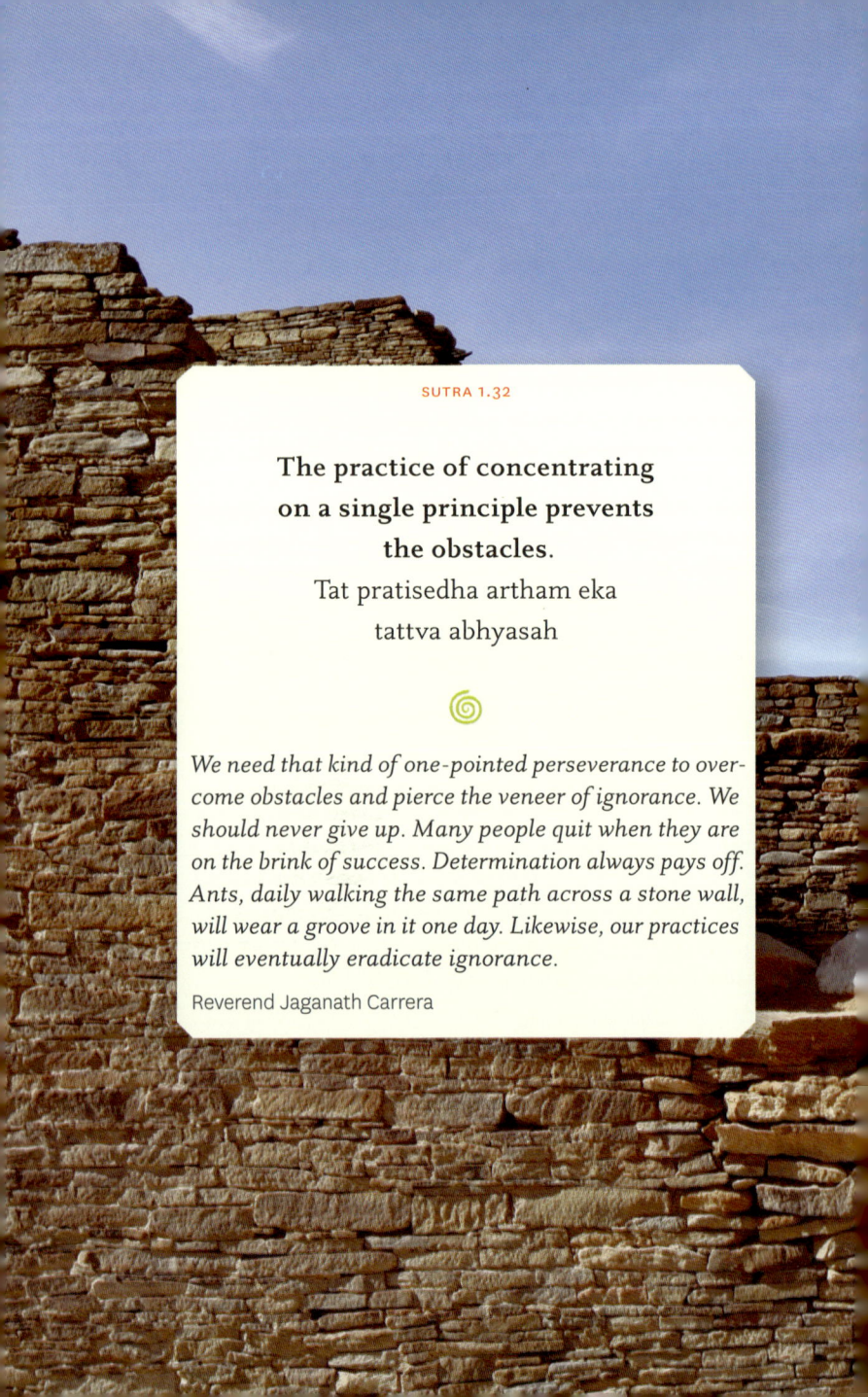

We need that kind of one-pointed perseverance to over-come obstacles and pierce the veneer of ignorance. We should never give up. Many people quit when they are on the brink of success. Determination always pays off. Ants, daily walking the same path across a stone wall, will wear a groove in it one day. Likewise, our practices will eventually eradicate ignorance.

Reverend Jaganath Carrera

**The mind becomes tranquil
through the practice of friendliness
toward the happy, compassion toward the
miserable, joy toward the
virtuous, and equanimity toward
the non-virtuous.**

Maitri karuna mudita upeksanam sukha
duhkha punya apunya visayanam
bhavanatas citta prasadanam

*Let us live happily then, not hating those who hate us!
Among men who hate us, let us dwell free from hatred.
Let us live happily then, free from ailments among the ailing!
Among men who are ailing, let us dwell free from ailments.
Let us live happily then, free from greed among the greedy!
Among men who are greedy, let us dwell free from greed.
Let us live happily then, though we call nothing our own.*

Lord Buddha, The Dhammapada: "Happiness"

Practices for Calming the Mind

Most of us think compulsively all the time; we talk to ourselves. If I talk all the time, I don't hear what anyone else has to say. In exactly the same way, if I think all the time, that is to say if I talk to myself all the time, I don't have anything to think about except thoughts. Therefore, I'm living entirely in the world of symbols, and I'm never in relationship with reality. I want to get in touch with reality. That's the basic reason for meditation.

Alan Watts

Let (the yogin) contemplate whatever object he desires. Having reached stability there, the mind-stuff reaches the stable state elsewhere also.

Vyasa

Patanjali described a variety of practices for calming our minds. These are meditating on objects, the heart center, enlightened sages, knowledge gained in dream experiences, or on any other spiritually uplifting object. Another practice is yogic breathing (*pranayama*). We are free to use any of these methods that are the most effective for us.

For example, one practice I use is to meditate on a spiritually uplifting object. I have a Buddha who lives almost hidden from view in the large wheat grasses just at the base of the palm tree in my backyard. If I spend just a few minutes every morning with my garden Buddha, I am rewarded with a feeling of calmness that I can carry throughout the day.

Patanjali makes the important point that Yoga is beneficial for everyone, regardless of their race, religion, or culture. As long as we are sincere and dedicated in our practice and the object of contemplation calms our minds, then we have Patanjali's blessing.

Or by the controlled exhalation and retention of the breath.

Pracchardana vidharanabhyam

va pranasya

Compressing the breathings, let him who has subdued all motions breathe forth through the nose with gentle breath. Let the wise man without fail restrain his mind, that chariot yoked with vicious horses. Let him perform his exercises in a place level, pure, free from pebbles, fire, and dust, delightful by its sounds, its water, and bowers, not painful to the eye and full of shelters and caves.

Svetasvatara Upanishad, Second Adhyaya, Verses 9–10

Or by concentrating on a sense object.

Visaya vati va pravrttir utpanna
manasah sthiti nibandhani

At times, when we are drinking tea with a friend, we are not aware of the tea or even of our friend sitting there. Practicing tea meditation is to be truly present with our tea and our friends. We recognize that we can dwell happily in the present moment despite all of our sorrows and worries. We sit there relaxed without having to say anything.

Thich Nhat Hanh

Or by meditating on the ever blissful inner light.

Visoka va jyotismati

When the light has risen, there is no day, no night, neither existence nor nonexistence.

Shiva alone is there.

That is the eternal, the adorable light of Savitri, and the ancient wisdom proceeded hence. His form cannot be seen; no one perceives him with the eye. Those who through heart and mind know him thus abiding in the heart become immortal.

Svetasvatara Upanishad, Chapter 4, Verses 18-20

Or by meditating on enlightened souls who are free from attachments to sense objects.

Vita raga visayam va cittam

If you want to be perfect, go, sell your possessions, and give to the poor, and you will have treasure in heaven. Then come follow me. Again, I tell you, it is easier for a camel to go through the eye of a needle than for a rich man to enter the kingdom of God.

Jesus Christ

Or by meditating on the knowledge gained from dreams and dreamless sleep.

Svapna nidra jñana alambanam va

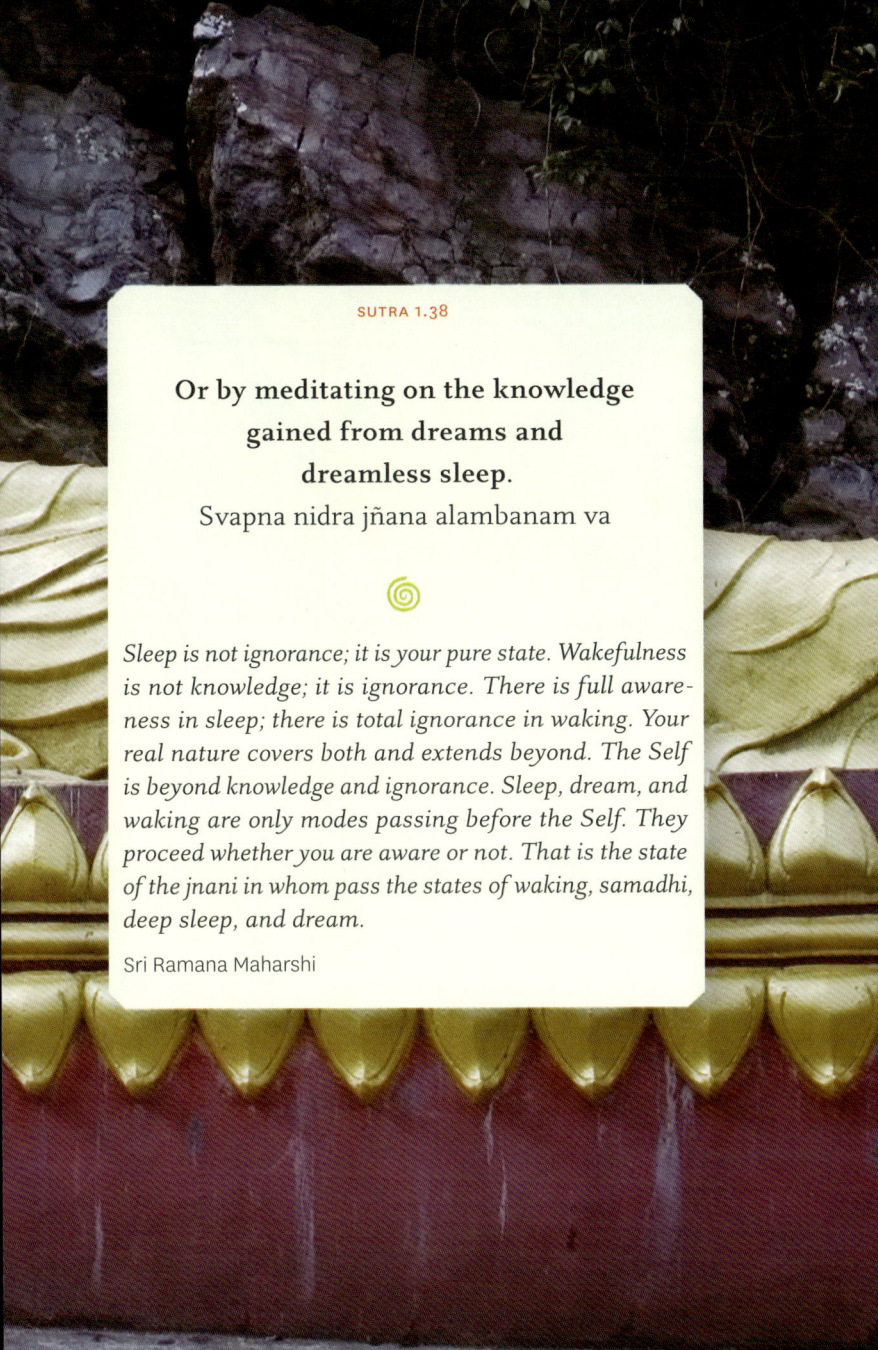

Sleep is not ignorance; it is your pure state. Wakefulness is not knowledge; it is ignorance. There is full awareness in sleep; there is total ignorance in waking. Your real nature covers both and extends beyond. The Self is beyond knowledge and ignorance. Sleep, dream, and waking are only modes passing before the Self. They proceed whether you are aware or not. That is the state of the jnani in whom pass the states of waking, samadhi, deep sleep, and dream.

Sri Ramana Maharshi

Or by meditating on any desirable object that is spiritually uplifting.

Yatha abhimata dhyanad va

[To remove the obstacles] *you could try a form of meditation that makes use of a visual object. For example, you can visualize something and then reflect on what it means to you. In India, we often meditate like this on the images of the gods. As we visualize a particular god in the mind's eye, we recite his or her name 108 or 1008 times, if we are following the tradition. This kind of meditation helps the mind to become quieter and more clear and prepares us for dhyana, the merging of the ego with the object of meditation.*

T. K. V. Desikachar

More Light on Samadhi

But those who are pure in heart, who practice meditation and conquer the senses and passions, shall attain the immortal Self, source of all light and source of all life.

The Mundaka Upanishad, Part I, Verse 11

Let us meditate on the shining Self,
Changeless, underlying the world of change,
And realized in the heart in samadhi.

The Tejabindu Upanishad, Verse 1

According to Sutra 1.17, the four stages of samadhi are *vitarka* (gross objects), *vicara* (more subtle objects), *ananda* (the state of joy and bliss), and *asmita* (the state of only the "I"). In this group of sutras, Patanjali subdivided vitarka and vicara samadhi into more subtle categories and sheds additional light on samadhi.

To expand our understanding of samadhi, we must explore Samkhya philosophy. The Yoga Sutras and Samkhya are intertwined much like strands of a rope. (Samkhya is discussed in the Introduction to Sutras 2.17–2.24 but a summary is presented below.) Samkhya is an ancient system of knowledge and is one of the six classical schools of Indian philosophy. The Sanskrit word *Samkhya* means "number," and the basic idea of the system is that the entire universe evolves out of twenty-five different principles or categories. These categories range from gross forms of matter (i.e., rocks) to the most subtle (i.e., mind) as well as pure awareness without form.

Out of these twenty-five categories, only two are considered to be fundamental and eternal. These are the basic cosmological principles which are known as *Purusha* and *Prakriti*. Put simply, Purusha is the unchanging, divine Self. Purusha is our true Self, which is pure and blissful consciousness. Purusha's nature is static and formless. It is considered the positive principle.

Prakriti, on the other hand, is perpetually changing nature, which is manifested in all forms, from the galaxies to the atoms to the quarks. Prakriti includes all levels of the mind. Prakriti's nature is dynamic and creative. It is life. We may think of Prakriti as including everything that is not Purusha. It is considered the negative principle.

Prakriti has three qualities known as the *gunas*. These are *sattva* (luminosity and lightness), *rajas* (activity), and *tamas* (darkness and heaviness). When the gunas are in a state of balance, Prakriti resides in an unmanifested, formless state. However, when this state of balance is disturbed by Purusha's awareness, Prakriti creates the universe by evolving from its beginning state of pure and subtle energy into progressively grosser states of matter.

One metaphor that is traditionally used to describe this process is that of the dancer and the spectator. Before the dance begins, the stage curtain is closed. The spectator sits in the audience in a state of passive awareness. The curtain comes up, the dancer appears, and the awareness of the spectator energizes the dancer into movement. The dancer creates all of the categories of matter in the universe by dancing it into existence. The spectator watches the dance but never participates in creation by dancing on the stage.

Prakriti first creates *chitta* (individual consciousness) and then intellect, ego, mind, cognitive and action faculties (i.e., sense organs and functions), subtle elements (i.e., sound, color), and last, the gross elements (i.e., space, air, fire, water, and earth). An easy way to think of Prakriti's creation of the universe is the movement from energy to consciousness to rocks. The interplay among Purusha, Prakriti, and the gunas involves complex philosophical matters that Yoga philosophers have debated for centuries.

The Yoga Sutras are based on the idea that our authentic or true Self is Purusha. Sutras 1.2 and 1.3 read together mean that when our minds are calm, the "seer" then resides in its true nature. The "seer" is a metaphor for pure awareness. The Yoga Sutras use Purusha to refer to this state. When our minds are not calm, they take on the form of the objects of perception (i.e., Prakriti). We become absorbed in what we are seeing or experiencing. This is a result of spiritual ignorance (i.e., avidya). In the state of spiritual ignorance, we mistake our true Self for the movements of our minds, and suffering is the result.

To state it in the language of Samkhya, our individual Purusha becomes entangled with Prakriti, and it mistakenly identifies with the endlessly changing forms of Prakriti. This case of mistaken identity is spiritual ignorance. Because Prakriti is impermanent and we are attached to the security that we think permanence will provide, suffering is the result.

We end suffering through our Yoga practice because we gain Yogic wisdom. This is known as viveka. Viveka is the ability to discriminate between our true Self and our ordinary minds, which are reflecting the endless movements of Prakriti. It is the ability to discriminate between Purusha and Prakriti. We resolve our spiritual ignorance by ending our mistaken identification with our ordinary minds and resting in Purusha, our true Self. Yogic wisdom is the solution to the suffering caused by spiritual ignorance.

Samadhi is the process of using meditation to work back from the gross elements to more and more subtle elements and states of mind until consciousness (Purusha) is free from its identification with

Prakriti. It is taking an inward journey back to the true Self, Purusha.

Samadhi is the unification of consciousness with the object or state that is being contemplated. It is the wisdom that is gained when the mind unifies with an object and grasps its innermost essence or nature. In samadhi we become aware of our original mind, which is vast like the sky: calm, blissful, and bright. By attaining deeper and deeper levels of viveka (spiritual wisdom), we end our spiritual ignorance (avidya) and realize our true Self.

Sutra 1.41 is a beautiful and instructive sutra that illuminates the basic idea behind samadhi. Sutra 1.41 states that when the modifications of the mind are under control, then it becomes naturally pure like a crystal. It reflects the knower, the known, and the act of knowing. If we place a red flower next to a crystal, the flower's color will be reflected in the crystal, and it will appear to be red. The crystal has not been changed in any way. It remains pure and transparent. The idea behind this sutra is to illustrate the point that the mind in its natural state is pure awareness. The innate nature of Purusha is not affected by its contact or interaction with the natural world of Prakriti because it is always just pure awareness.

In the same way, our true Self (our Purusha) takes the form of the external world or emotional states that it is perceiving. We may become completely immersed in our emotions, our life story, or in our senses. However, our true Self remains pure awareness, and it is not affected by these external forms or emotional states. By the same token, if we concentrate our minds on such things as the inner light, enlightened souls, or spiritual objects, our true Self (Purusha) takes the form of these things and becomes calm. This is the state of samadhi. Of course, in the highest states of samadhi, even these things are left behind and we reside in our true Self, the state of pure awareness.

Mastery of concentration may extend from the smallest particle to the infinite.

Parama anu parama mahatva anta asya vasikarah

The mind by this practice easily contemplates the most minute thing as well as the biggest thing. Thus the mind waves become fainter.

Sri Swami Vivekananda

When the fluctuations (vrttis) of the mind are under control, the mind becomes like a naturally pure crystal, reflecting the knower, the known, and the act of knowing. This is samadhi.

Ksina vrtter abhijatasya iva
maner grahitr grahana grahyesu tat
stha tad añjanata samapattih

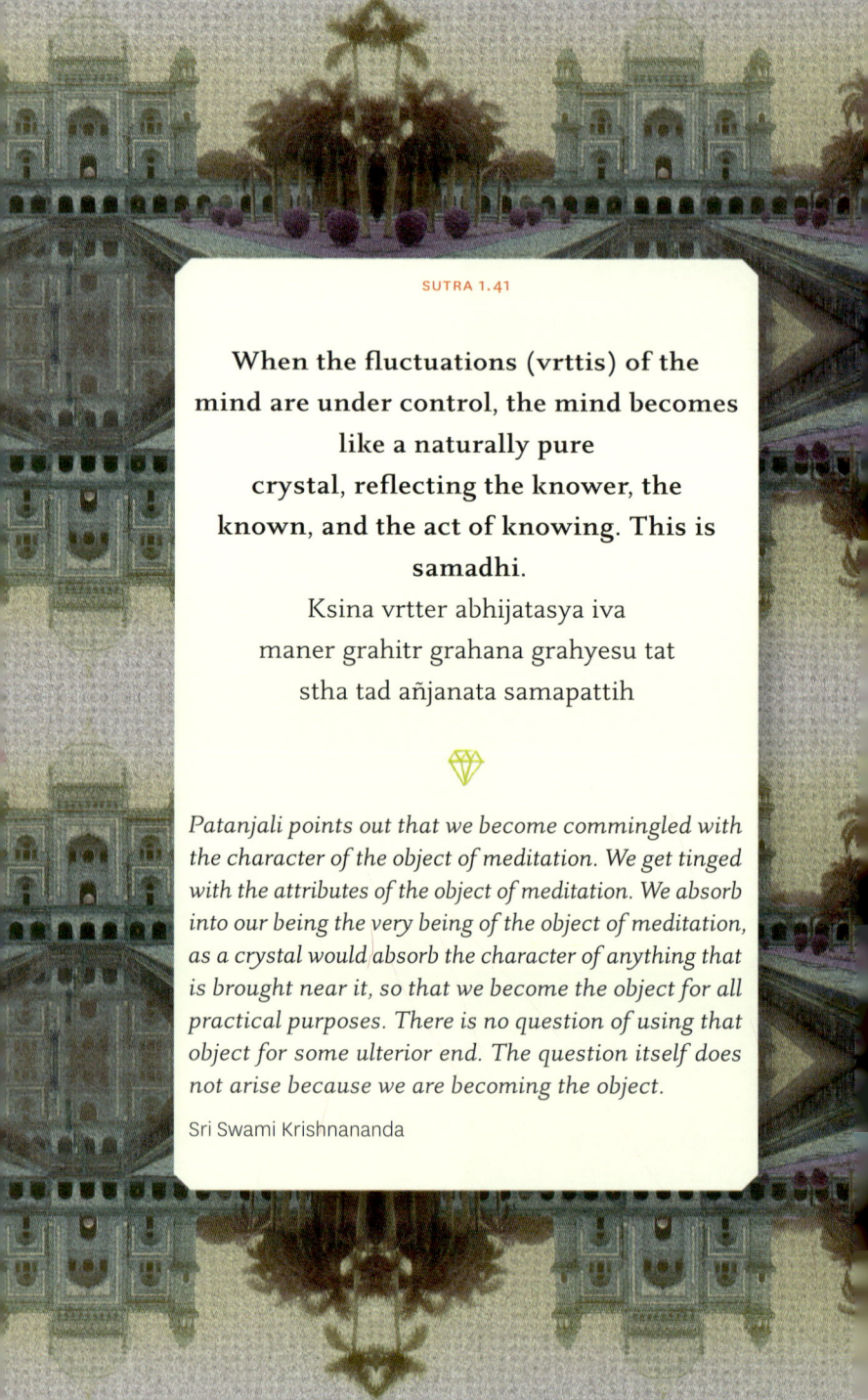

Patanjali points out that we become commingled with the character of the object of meditation. We get tinged with the attributes of the object of meditation. We absorb into our being the very being of the object of meditation, as a crystal would absorb the character of anything that is brought near it, so that we become the object for all practical purposes. There is no question of using that object for some ulterior end. The question itself does not arise because we are becoming the object.

Sri Swami Krishnananda

**When the name of an object,
the meaning of an object,
and knowledge of the object are mixed,
the state of savitarka samapatti
is reached.**

Tatra sabda artha jñana vikalpaih
samkirna savitarka samapattih

A realized being holds an apple in the hand but not in the mind.

Baba Hari Dass

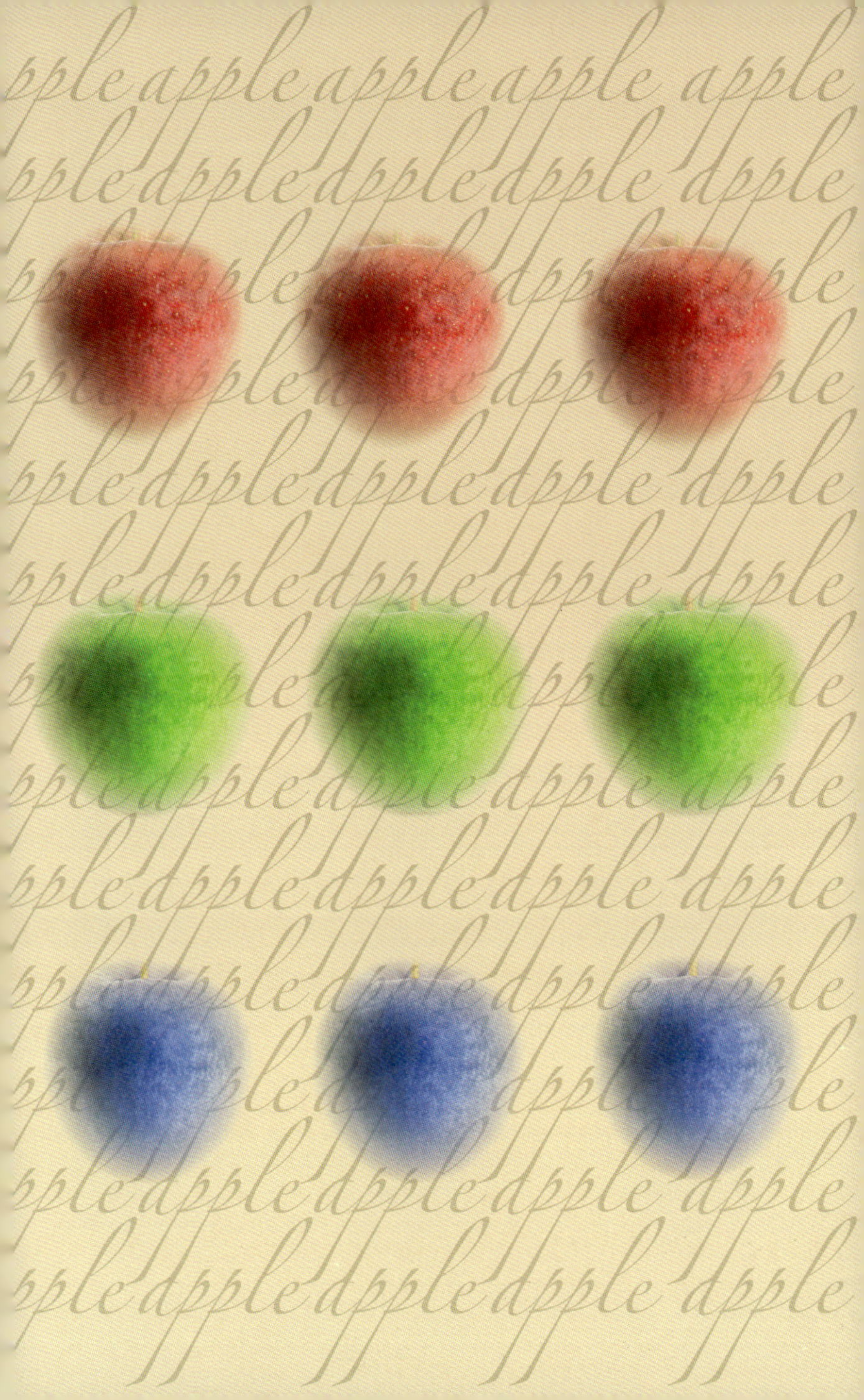

**Nirvitarka samapatti is attained
when memory is completely
purified and the mind becomes empty and
sees the true nature of things.**

Smrti parisuddhau sva rupa sunya iva artha
matra nirbhasa nirvitarka

*The dharma of Thusness is intimately transmitted by
Buddhas. Now you have it; preserve it well. A silver bowl
filled with snow; a heron hidden in the moon. Taken
as similar, they are not the same; not distinguished,
their places are known. The meaning does not reside
in the words, but a pivotal moment brings it forth. In
darkest night, it is perfectly clear; in the light of dawn,
it is hidden. Like facing a precious mirror: form and
reflection hold each other.*

You are not it, but in truth it is you.

Tung-shan Liang-chieh

The other two types of contemplation on subtle objects, savicara (reflective) and nirvacara (non-reflective), are therefore explained.

Etaya eva savicara nirvicara ca suksma visaya vyakhyata

Empty yourself of everything.
Let the mind rest at peace.
The ten thousand things rise and fall while
the Self watches their return.
They grow and flourish and then
return to the source.
Returning to the source is stillness,
which is the way of nature.

Lao Tzu

The most subtle objects end with unmanifested nature (Prakriti).

Suksma visayatvam ca alinga paryavasanam

Prakriti is the elemental, undifferentiated stuff of matter, the energy by which all phenomena are projected. As the meditative mind turns inward, it probes through the gross outer coverings of things to their subtle essences; and beyond these subtle essences, it comes to Prakriti itself. But Prakriti is not the ultimate Reality. Behind Prakriti is Brahman. The four kinds of samadhi already described are all within the realm of phenomena, and they are only preparations for that state of direct union with Brahman, which is the highest samadhi of all.

Christopher Isherwood

These (savitarka, nirvitarka, savicara, and nirvicara samadhi) are samadhis with seed.

Ta eva sabijah samadhih

That is, seeds of desire and attachment may still remain within the mind, even though perfect concentration has been achieved. And these seeds of desire are dangerous, as we saw in considering the fate of those who concentrate without nonattachment. However, liberation is now very near. The aspirant has already risen to such heights that it is unlikely that he will fall back into bondage.

Christopher Isherwood

On attaining the clarity of nirvicara samadhi, there is the dawning of the spiritual light of the true Self.

Nirvicara vaisaradya adhyatmam prasadah

This realization may take many forms. A simple one is something like this: You might be looking at a mountain, and you have relaxed into effortlessness of your own present awareness, and then suddenly the mountain is all, you are nothing. Your separate-self sense is suddenly and totally gone, and there is simply everything that is arising moment to moment. You are perfectly aware, perfectly conscious, everything seems completely normal, except you are nowhere to be found. You are not on this side of your face looking at the mountain out there; you simply are the mountain, you are the sky, you are the clouds, you are everything that is arising moment to moment, very simply, very clearly, just so.

Ken Wilber

On Truth Bearing Insight:
Rtambhara Prajna

By truth, meditation, and self-control
One can enter into this state of joy
And see the Self shining in a pure heart.
Truth is victorious, never untruth.
Truth is the way; truth is the goal of life,
Reached by sages who are free from self-will.

Mundaka Upanishad, Part III, Verses 5–6

In these final sutras of Pada One, Patanjali describes the state of *rtambhara prajna* and *nirbija samadhi*. Rtambhara prajna is the truth-bearing insight associated with the highest levels of samadhi. It is a direct experience of the true Self that transcends the everyday mind.

As we have seen, this is different from knowledge gained from the study of books, our senses, or our intellect. Sri Swami Satchidananda explains as follows: "Experiencing God is something that is genuine and comes only when you transcend the mind. God cannot be understood by the mind, because mind is matter, and matter cannot possibly understand something more subtle than the mind."

Patanjali describes the highest level of samadhi which is nirbija samadhi. In this state, the mind is free from all objects, ideas, and symbols. The universe and the self merge into oneness. There is complete union with the divine consciousness, which is our true Self.

This state is beautifully expressed in the Upanishads: "To be united with the Lord of Love is to be freed from all conditioning. This is the state of Self-realization, far beyond the reach of words or thoughts."

In that state is truth bearing wisdom.

Rtam bhara tatra prajna

Yet meditation will truly calm the mind, fill the heart with joy, and bring peace to the soul; the serenity and joy last throughout the day and throughout your life. Meditation is not a simple diversion which works only as long as you are actively engaged in it. Rather, meditation brings you into contact with God; it changes the very nature of your being. As you sit in meditation, you will realize the insignificance of that which causes anxiety; you will realize the transient nature of all your troubles. You will realize the infinite joy and boundless peace that come from God.

H. H. Pujya Swami Chidanand Saraswatiji

This wisdom is beyond knowledge gained by tradition, testimony, or inference.

Sruta anumana prajnabhyam anya visaya visesa arthatvat

When Buddha was in Grdhrakuta mountain he turned a flower in his fingers and held it before his listeners. Every one was silent. Only Maha-Kashapa smiled at this revelation, although he tried to control the lines of his face.

Buddha said: "I have the eye of the true teaching, the heart of Nirvana, the true aspect of non-form, and the ineffable stride of Dharma. It is not expressed by words, but especially transmitted beyond teaching. This teaching I have given to Maha-Kashapa."

The Gateless Gate-Buddha Twirls a Flower

As this wisdom strengthens, all previous mental impressions (samskaras) are left behind, and the formation of other samskaras is obstructed.

Tajjah samskarah anya samskara pratibandhi

The impression that results from the samadhi by which you get ritambhara prajna will obstruct all other impressions. Everything dies away, and there is no more coming back as an ordinary person, ignorant of your true nature. When you come to this stage, you always retain this knowledge. In this state you become a jivanmukta, a realized saint. "Jivan" means one who lives; "mukta" means liberated. So such a person is a liberated living being. You live, eat, and talk like anybody else, even do business like anybody else, but still you are liberated.

Sri Swami Satchidananda

稲葉山の月

When even that wisdom ends, seedless samadhi dawns.

Tasya api nirodhe sarva nirodhan nirbijah samadhih

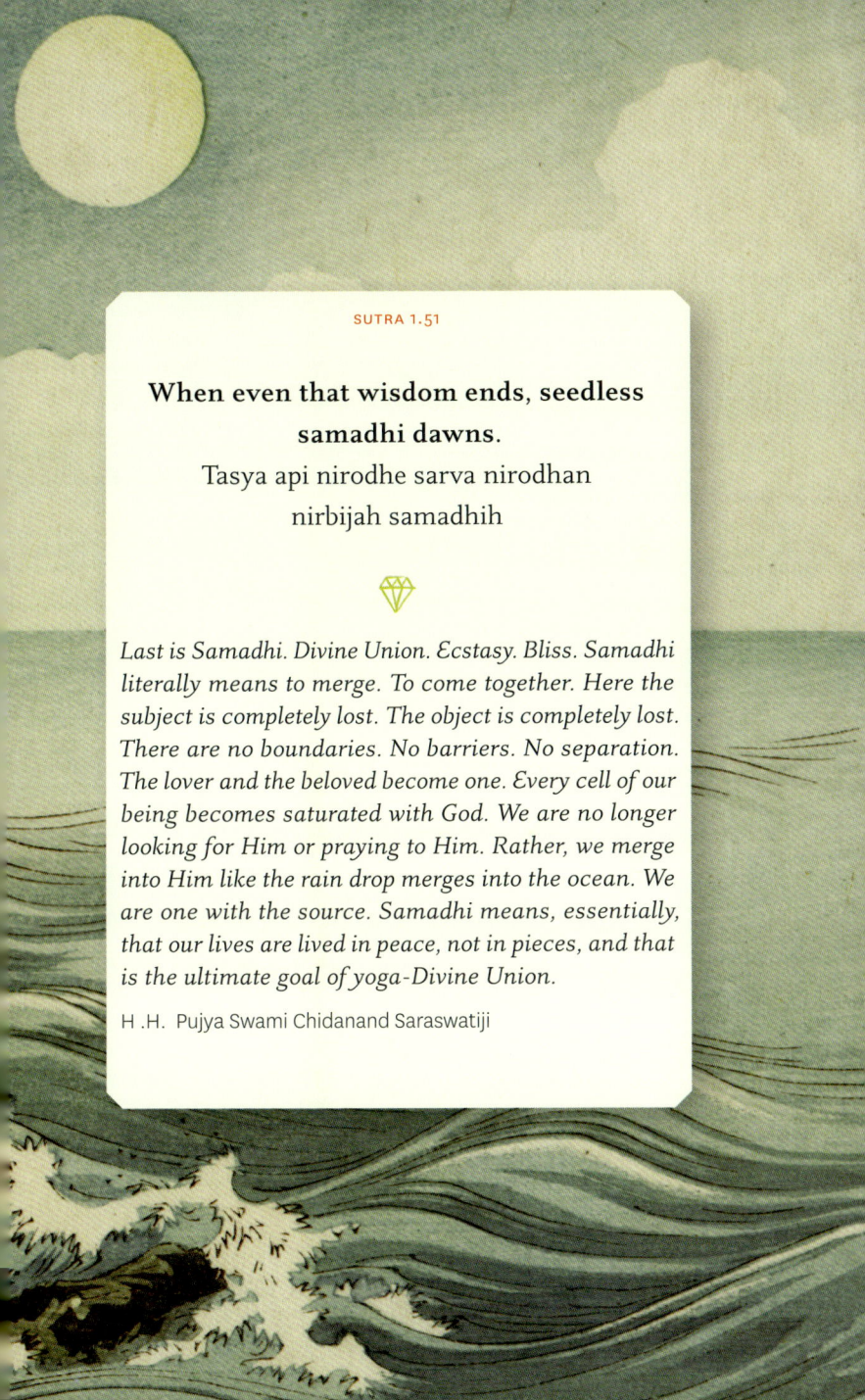

Last is Samadhi. Divine Union. Ecstasy. Bliss. Samadhi literally means to merge. To come together. Here the subject is completely lost. The object is completely lost. There are no boundaries. No barriers. No separation. The lover and the beloved become one. Every cell of our being becomes saturated with God. We are no longer looking for Him or praying to Him. Rather, we merge into Him like the rain drop merges into the ocean. We are one with the source. Samadhi means, essentially, that our lives are lived in peace, not in pieces, and that is the ultimate goal of yoga-Divine Union.

H .H. Pujya Swami Chidanand Saraswatiji

Afterword to Pada One

Even though the man sees the world after he has been in the samadhi state, the world will be taken only at its worth, that is to say it is the phenomenon of the One Reality. The True Being can be realised only in samadhi; what was then is also now. Otherwise it cannot be Reality or Ever-present Being. What was in samadhi is here and now too. Hold it and it is your natural condition of Being. Samadhi practice must lead to it. Otherwise how can nirvikalpa samadhi be of any use in which a man remains as a log of wood? He must necessarily rise up from it sometime or other and face the world. But in sahaja samadhi he remains unaffected by the world.

So many pictures pass over the cinema screen: fire burns away everything, water drenches all, but the screen remains unaffected. The scenes are only phenomena which pass away leaving the screen as it was. Similarly the world phenomena simply pass on before the Jnani, leaving him unaffected.

You may say that people find pain or pleasure in worldly phenomena. It is owing to superimposition. This must not happen. With this end in view, practice is made. Practice lies in one of the two courses: devotion or knowledge.

Even these are not the goals. Samadhi must be gained; it must be continuously practised until sahaja samadhi results. Then there remains nothing more to do.

Sri Ramana Maharshi

Sadhana Pada

Sadhana means a discipline undertaken in pursuit of a spiritual goal. It includes a variety of practices. The Sadhana Pada was written for those of us who are just beginning our journey on the path of Yoga. The Samadhi Pada, on the other hand, was written for those who are more spiritually advanced. Patanjali began the Yoga Sutras with the Samadhi Pada because he wanted to establish the goal of Yoga and then give us practices to accomplish that goal.

In the Sadhana Pada, Patanjali gave us two different systems of Yoga. These are Kriya Yoga and Astanga Yoga. Scholars of the Yoga Sutras believe that Kriya Yoga is Patanjali's unique creation and that Astanga Yoga is a compilation of practices from historical sources.

Kriya Yoga is the three-limbed practice consisting of *tapas, svadhyaya* and *Isvara pranidhanani*. Tapas is the self-discipline and hard work that we need to have a successful Yoga practice. It also suggests the purification that comes from the spiritual heat of a dedicated practice. Svadhyaya is the study of spiritual works. It also means self-study. Isvara pranidhanani is devotion or surrender to Isvara, the Supreme Being. It is dedicating the fruits of our actions to Isvara without the intention of getting anything in return.

Astanga Yoga is the "eight limbs" of Yoga. These limbs are the great vows (*yamas*), the observances (*niyamas*), postures (*asana*), regulation of breath (*pranayama*), withdrawal of the senses (*pratyaharah*), concentration (*dharana*), meditation (*dhyana*), and absorption (*samadhi*).

The first five limbs of Astanga Yoga are known as the external practices because they primarily concern our relationship with the external world and our bodies. The remaining three limbs are internal because they are meditational practices that lead us to samadhi. These limbs are addressed in Pada Three.

The Sadhana Pada also contains the philosophy of the klesas. The klesas are sometimes known as the poisons of the mind because they cause our suffering. The root word *klis* means "to torment, trouble, cause pain, or to afflict." The klesas are spiritual ignorance (*avidya*), ego (*asmita*), attachment (*raga*), aversion (*dvesa*), and clinging to bodily life (*abhinivesah*). Spiritual ignorance is the most important klesa because it is the soil from which the rest of the klesas grow like weeds.

The klesas are an obstacle to our Yoga practice because they cause suffering and disturb our minds. As we have seen, the goal of Yoga-as stated in Sutras 1.2 and 1.3- is to calm our minds so that we can reside in our true Self. We must therefore eliminate the klesas to reach our goal.

In Sutra 2.2 Patanjali taught that the practice of Kriya Yoga destroys the klesas and leads us to samadhi. Through the practice of Yoga we attain *viveka* which is spiritual wisdom. Because wisdom is the antidote to ignorance, our minds are no longer poisoned by the klesas and we can realize our goals.

Kriya Yoga and the Philosophy of the Klesas

Those who set their hearts on me and worship me with unfailing devotion and faith are more established in Yoga.

Bhagavad Gita, Chapter 12, Verse 2

Kriya Yoga is based upon three core practices: discipline (tapas), study (svadhyaya), and devotion (Isvara pranidhanani). The first practice is tapas. It is often translated as "heat." Its yogic meaning may have originated by observing the process of heating gold ore to burn off its impurities so that only the pure gold is left behind. Tapas suggests the self-discipline that is needed to actively pursue and attain our spiritual goals. We purify our bodies and minds through the inner heat that is created as we pursue our Yoga practice with intensity and self-discipline. We have all felt the resistance and excuse-making that arise as we debate whether to attend that early Saturday morning Yoga class: it's too early, we are too busy, or we indulged ourselves at last night's party. The practice of tapas can encourage us to make that extra effort to get to class and to practice with mindfulness and energy.

Most of us have experienced tapas in our asana practice. We have all felt those burning sensations in our bodies when our teachers have instructed us to hold a pose longer than we may wish. Even though this may be painful at the time, we are building physical strength. After a particularly long and intense Yoga class, we often feel emotionally and physically purified.

Sally Kempton, a contemporary meditation teacher, describes how the practice of tapas can be used to purify our minds:

Meditation and mindfulness practice teach us to sit through bore-dom, mental restlessness, and emotional upheavals. Another form of tapas is the effort we make to tell the truth, practice kindness and non-violence. But during hard times, tapas often means pure endur-ance—hanging tight when fear, sadness, and frustration threaten to send us into a tailspin. Doing tapas, we actually become heirs to the great spiritual practitioners who experienced long periods of difficulty, doubt, and darkness, figures like St. John of the Cross,

Ramakrishna, and Bodhidharma—especially if, like them, we also remember to practice self-study and surrender."

Kempton refers to this as "the alchemical power of adversity."

The second element of Kriya Yoga is svadhyaya. Svadhyaya means study of scriptures. This includes the knowledge gained through the recitation of mantras such as OM as well as the study of spiritual scriptures. Patanjali does not require that we study scriptures from any specific spiritual tradition. Rather, we only need to study scriptures that inspire us and prepare us for the deeper insights that we gain as we progress along the spiritual path. Scriptures may be such writings as the Vedas, the Upanishads, the Yoga Sutras, the Bhagavad Gita, the Torah, the Dhammapada, the Tao Te Ching, the Bible, or the Koran.

The third element of Kriya Yoga is Isvara pranidhanani. Isvara means "Supreme Being," and pranidhanani means "surrender." Surrendering to a Supreme Being is the action of letting go of our personal desires and goals and accepting whatever is given to us by the Supreme Being. It also means dedicating the fruits of our actions to the Supreme Being or to benefit another person without any thought of personal gain. Sri Pujya Swami Chidanand Saraswatiji explains this beautifully as follows:

One of the greatest sources of depression and discontent is our inability to accept situations which befall us. We try to impose our will onto every situation. We try to sculpt the world into our own preconceived image of what is right, as though we were appointed as the Great Divine Sculptor, given the task of ensuring that everything conformed to the correct mold. However, we were not appointed as such, nor has anyone been given the Divine Vision to know the Divine Plan. Thus, for us to take on the task of trying to make the world conform to our will is not only futile but it ensures that our lives will be frustrating, unfruitful, and marked by perspiration rather than inspiration! The only way to live peacefully, with joy and bliss, and to fulfill your individual dharma here on Earth is to allow God's will rather than your own will to guide you.

In Sutra 2.2, Patanjali states that the goal of Kriya Yoga is to eliminate the klesas and attain samadhi. The klesas are known as the afflictions. They obstruct our progress on the path of Yoga and are the source of suffering. The afflictions are spiritual ignorance (avidya), ego (asmita), attachment (raga), aversion (dvesa), and clinging to bodily life (abhinivesah). Sally Kempton explains as follows:

The klesas make us imagine that we're separate from others and the universe. They delude us into identifying ourselves with our bodies and personalities, trying to pleasure our made-up self and to avoid anything that gives pain. They keep us in perpetual fear of annihilation.

The most important klesa is spiritual ignorance because it is the soil from which all the other klesas grow. Fundamentally, spiritual ignorance is a condition in which we have forgotten our true nature as divine consciousness. Because we are spiritually ignorant, we identify with the impermanent and changing world and the fluctuations of our minds rather than with our true Self. In this condition, no peace is possible because it is as if we are attempting to build a house on sand. When we overcome the klesas through the practice of Kriya Yoga-discipline, study, and surrender to the Supreme Being-we naturally experience the peace and joy that is our true nature.

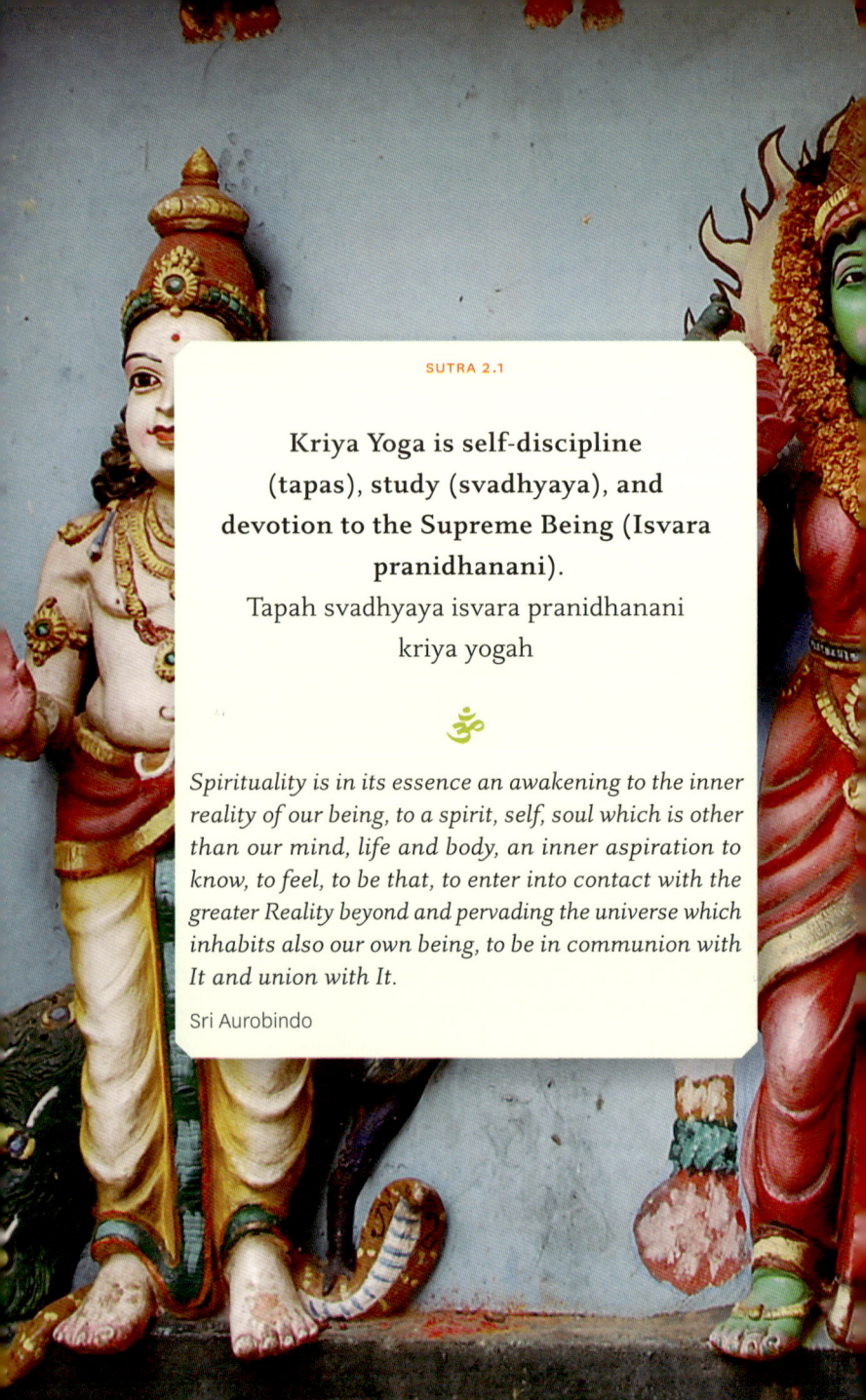

Kriya Yoga is self-discipline (tapas), study (svadhyaya), and devotion to the Supreme Being (Isvara pranidhanani).

Tapah svadhyaya isvara pranidhanani kriya yogah

ॐ

Spirituality is in its essence an awakening to the inner reality of our being, to a spirit, self, soul which is other than our mind, life and body, an inner aspiration to know, to feel, to be that, to enter into contact with the greater Reality beyond and pervading the universe which inhabits also our own being, to be in communion with It and union with It.

Sri Aurobindo

Tapas

Tapas is what produces heat. It stirs energy or power within the Yogin. The practice of Brahmacharya (i.e., moderation) and of the Yamas in general stimulates supernatural power. The Yamas (i.e., the moral vows) themselves constitute an intense Tapas. In a broad sense, moderateness in life may be said to constitute Tapas. Sense-control is Tapas. To speak sweetly, and not hurtingly, is Tapas. To eat a little is Tapas. To sleep less is Tapas. Not to exhibit animal qualities is Tapas. To be humane is Tapas. To be good and to do good is Tapas. Tapas is mental, verbal, or physical. Calmness of mind and subdued emotions form mental Tapas. Sweet but truthful speech is verbal Tapas. Unselfish service to others is physical Tapas.

Sri Swami Krishnananda

Svadhyaya

Svadhyaya is principally a disciplined study of such texts as deal with the way of the salvation of the soul. This Niyama (i.e., the observances) helps the student in maintaining a psychic contact with the masters who have given these holy writings.

When one reads the Bhagavad Gita, for example, not merely does one gather knowledge of a high order, but one also establishes an inner contact with Bhagavan Sri Krishna and Maharshi Vyasa. Svadhyaya is continued persistence in study of a scripture of Yoga.

Sri Swami Krishnananda

Isvara Pranidhanani

To dwell in the joy that springs from the mind's constant occupation with things divine is man's duty. Thinking of anything other than God is what creates sorrow. Be it mantra japa, be it meditation, worship, perusal of sacred texts, the simple awareness of God or a like device, be it kirtan or religious music—all these are different modes of being in the divine Presence. One should always remain engaged in one of them, in fact never be without Him.

Sri Anandamayi Ma

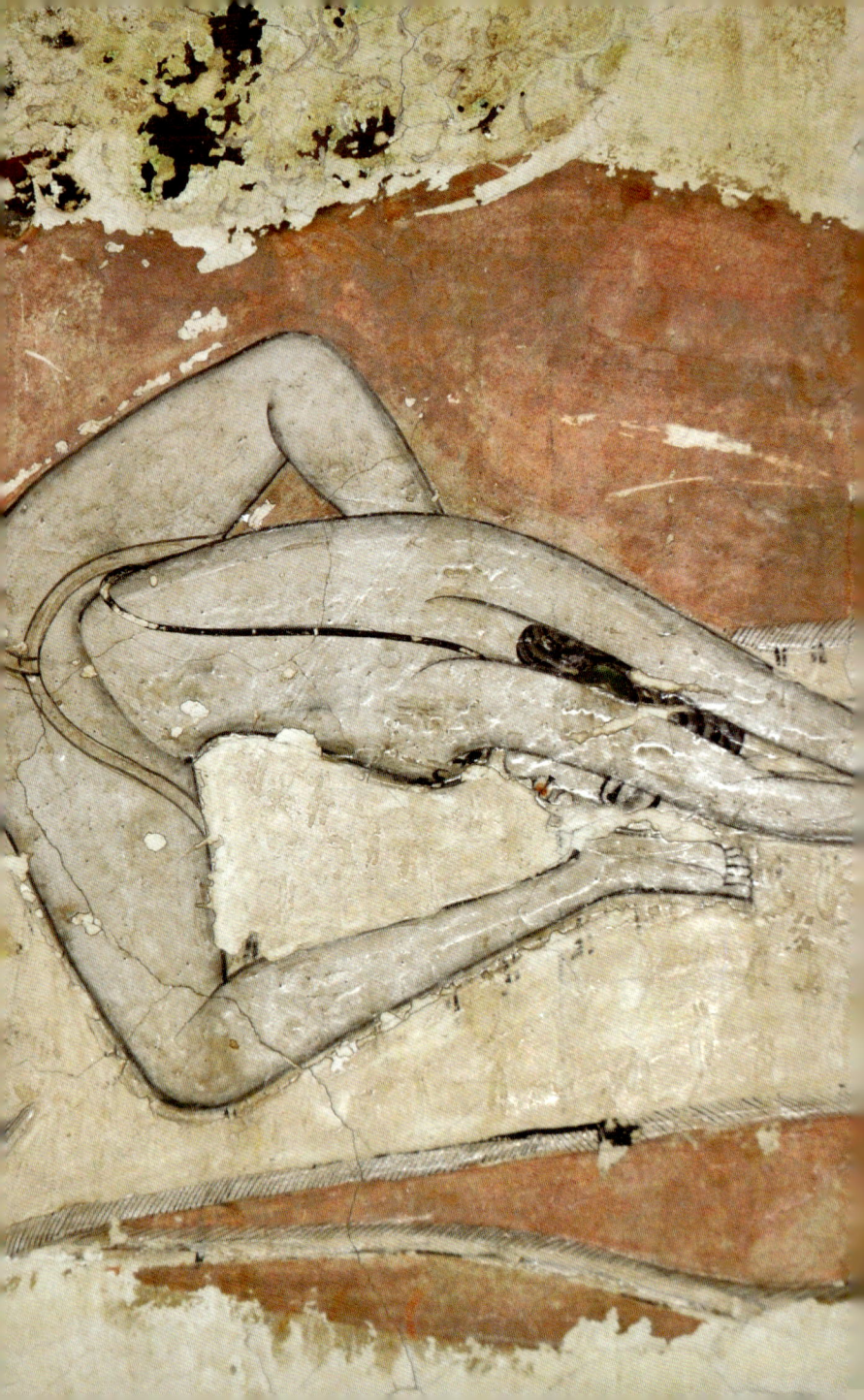

**The practice of Kriya Yoga reduces
the afflictions (klesas) and
leads toward samadhi.**

Samadhi bhavana arthah klesa tanu
karana arthas ca samadhi

*In all my deeds may I probe into my mind,
And as soon as mental
and emotional afflictions arise—
As they endanger myself and others—
May I strongly confront them and avert them.*

H. H. The Dalai Lama

The klesas are spiritual ignorance
(avidya), egoism (asmita),
attachment (raga), aversion (dvesa), and
clinging to life (abhinivesah).
Avidya asmita raga dvesa abhinivesah
panca klesah

*We do not know Universal Being. We know only the
particular and the individual. We love and hate objects.
We cling to life and fear death. The first mistake is to
think, 'I am not the Universal'; the second to affirm, 'I
am the particular'; the third to like certain things and
to dislike others; the fourth to strive for perpetuating
individuality by the instinct for self-preservation. We
have now to wake up from this muddled thinking and
go back to the truth of thinking universally. The union
of the individual with the Universal is Yoga.*

Sri Swami Krishnananda

**Spiritual ignorance (avidya) is
the cause of the other klesas,
whether they are dormant, weak,
interrupted, or sustained.**
Avidya ksetram uttaresam prasupta
tanu vicchinna udaranam

*Learned is one who can distinguish between the Self and
the mind. Ignorant is one who identifies with the body.*

Baba Hari Dass

**Avidya (spiritual ignorance)
is regarding the impermanent as
permanent, the impure as pure,
the painful as pleasant, and the
non-self as the Self.**

Anitya asuci duhkha anatmasu nitya
suci sukha atma khyatir avidya

*Ignorance ... is false identification. It is a misunder-
standing of one's real nature. If you say, "I am this
body, which is named Patanjali," you are regarding
the non-Atman (i.e., the body and mind) as the Atman
(i.e., the true Self). By denying the Atman within us,
we deny it everywhere. We misread Nature. We dwell
on the outwardness of things and see the universe as
multiplicity, not unity.*

*Instead of eternity, we cling to what seems relatively
enduring. Instead of true happiness, we clutch at what
seems temporarily pleasant. But, also, our satisfac-
tion is short-lived. The strongest tower falls, the most
beautiful flower withers in our hands. . . .*

Christopher Isherwood

Egoism is the identification of the Seer (Purusha) with the instruments of seeing.

Drg darsana saktyor eka atmata
iva asmita

We are all looking for the peace and freedom and security of perfect union with the Atman. We all long desperately to be happy. But ignorance misdirects us. It assures us that the Atman cannot really be within us, that we are nothing but individuals, separate egos. And so we start to search for this dimly conceived, eternal happiness amidst the finite and transient phenomena of the external world. Like the fabled musk deer, we search all over the earth for that haunting fragrance which is really exuded from ourselves. We stumble, we hurt ourselves, we endure endless hardships—but we never look in the right place.

Christopher Isherwood

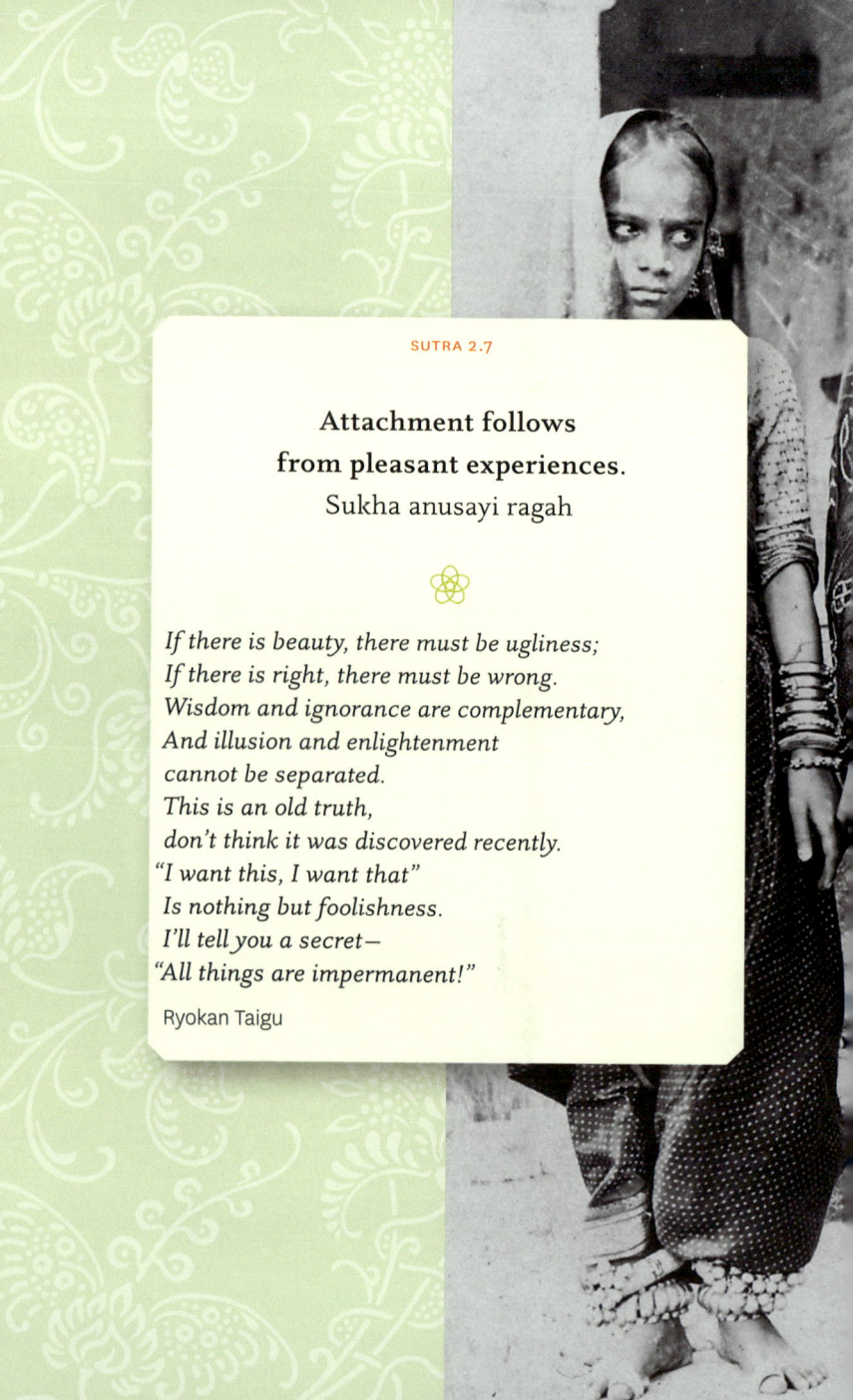

Attachment follows
from pleasant experiences.

Sukha anusayi ragah

If there is beauty, there must be ugliness;
If there is right, there must be wrong.
Wisdom and ignorance are complementary,
And illusion and enlightenment
cannot be separated.
This is an old truth,
don't think it was discovered recently.
"I want this, I want that"
Is nothing but foolishness.
I'll tell you a secret—
"All things are impermanent!"

Ryokan Taigu

Aversion follows
from painful experiences.
Duhkha anusayi dvesah

To set up what you like
against what you dislike—
This is the disease of the mind:
When the deep meaning
of the Way is not understood
Peace of mind is disturbed
and nothing is gained.

Third Ch'an Patriarch Chien-chih Seng-ts'an

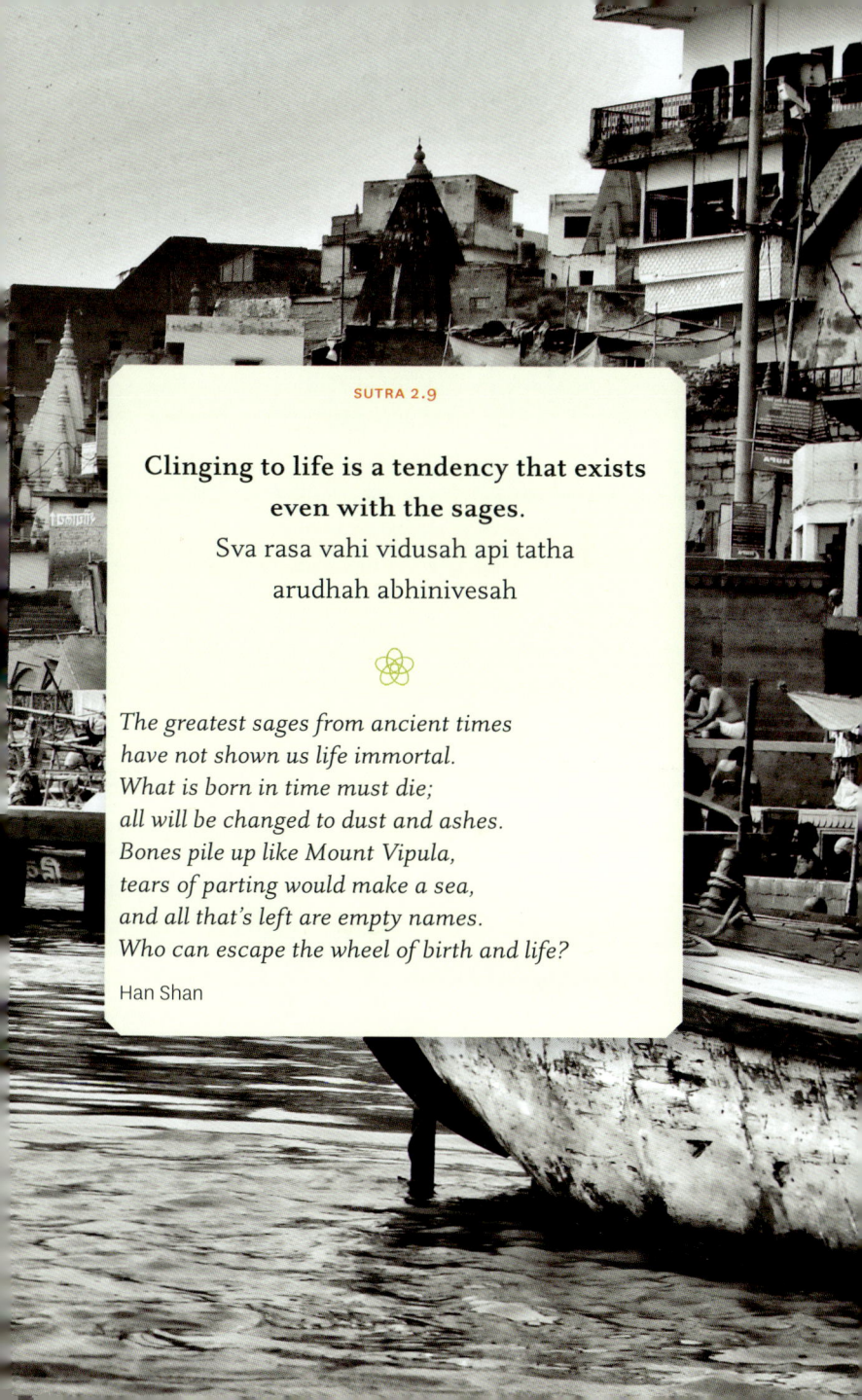

Clinging to life is a tendency that exists even with the sages.

Sva rasa vahi vidusah api tatha
arudhah abhinivesah

The greatest sages from ancient times
have not shown us life immortal.
What is born in time must die;
all will be changed to dust and ashes.
Bones pile up like Mount Vipula,
tears of parting would make a sea,
and all that's left are empty names.
Who can escape the wheel of birth and life?

Han Shan

**Pratiprasava is overcoming the
five afflictions in their subtle form
by resolving them backwards
to their origin.**

Te pratiprasava heyah suksmah

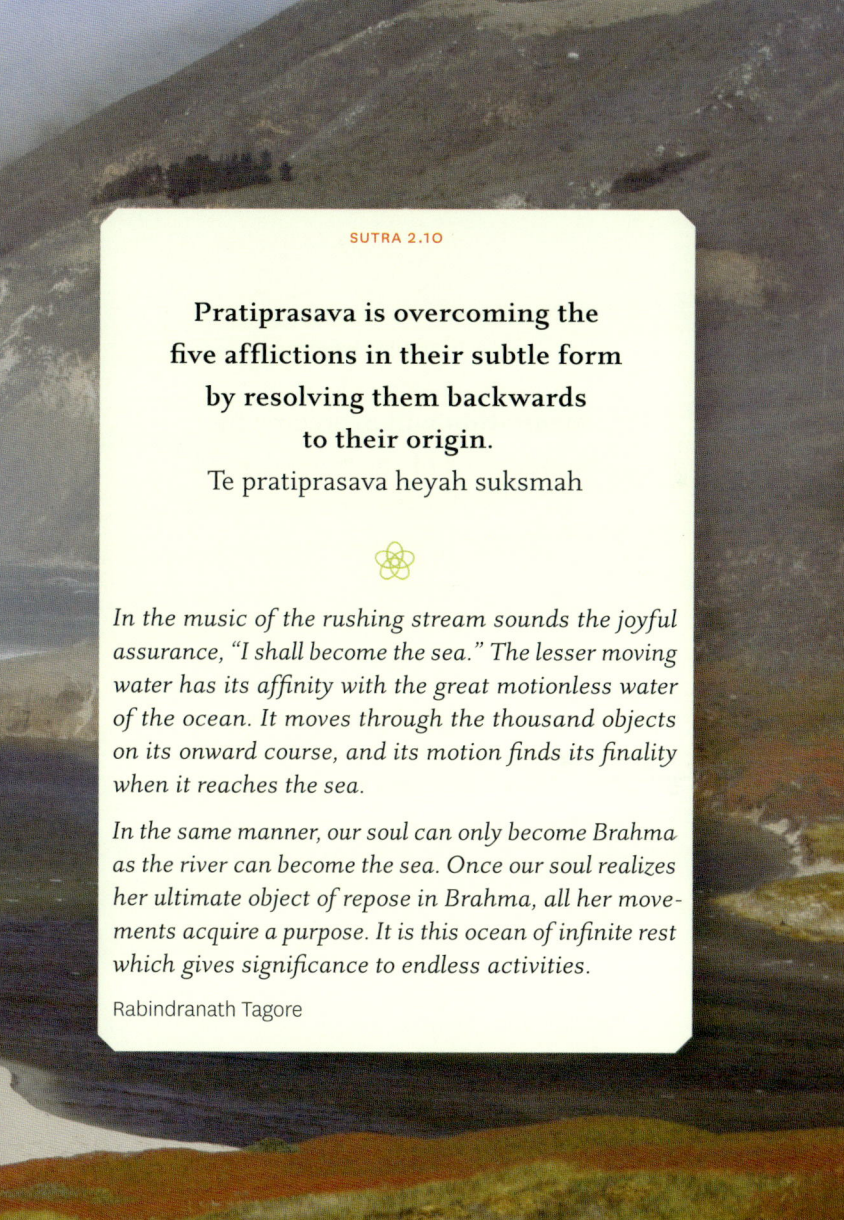

*In the music of the rushing stream sounds the joyful
assurance, "I shall become the sea." The lesser moving
water has its affinity with the great motionless water
of the ocean. It moves through the thousand objects
on its onward course, and its motion finds its finality
when it reaches the sea.*

*In the same manner, our soul can only become Brahma
as the river can become the sea. Once our soul realizes
her ultimate object of repose in Brahma, all her movements acquire a purpose. It is this ocean of infinite rest
which gives significance to endless activities.*

Rabindranath Tagore

Meditation will overcome the fluctuations of the mind caused by the afflictions.

Dhyana heyas tad vrttayah

The practice of meditation frees one from all affliction. This is the path of Yoga. Follow it with determination and sustained enthusiasm. Renouncing wholeheartedly all selfish desires and expectations, use your will to control the senses. Little by little, through patience and repeated effort, the mind will become stilled in the Self.

Bhagavad Gita, Chapter 6, Verses 23–24

Karma and the Klesas

I'll come right out and say it. The Soul transcends death, and we're reincarnated. That's what I believe. We're learning so that eventually we can become a Buddha, reach Heaven, or enter into union with the Divine. To be here for fifty or eighty years only to be annihilated at the end just doesn't make sense. Nothing else in the universe is that inefficient. We have to be here to learn; otherwise, our difficulties are truly meaningless.

Ram Dass

Each human soul goes through a continuous series of incarnations, reaping the fruits of thoughts, desires, and actions done in the past and generating, during the process of reaping, new causes which will bear their fruits in this or future lives. So every human life is like a flowing current in which two processes are at work simultaneously, the working out of Karmas made in the past and the generation of new Karmas which will bear fruit in the future. Each thought, desire, emotion, and action produces its corresponding result with mathematical exactitude, and this result is recorded naturally and automatically in our life's ledger.

I. K. Taimni

In Sutras 2.12–2.14 Patanjali described the related laws of karma and reincarnation. Yoga philosophy adopts the principle that the soul is immortal and is reborn after the death of the body. Each soul is caught in a cycle of birth, death, and rebirth that is known as *samsara*. This process is driven by the law of karma. The ultimate goal of Yoga is to escape from the cycle of samsara by liberating the soul so that it will not be continuously reborn.

Karma means action. It refers to the universal principles of cause and effect, action and reaction, which govern all life. According to the Vedas, if one sows goodness, one will reap goodness; if one sows evil, one will reap evil.

This has also been expressed in the Bible in Galatians 6:7–8 as follows: "Do not be deceived, God cannot be mocked. A man reaps what he sows. The one who sows to please his sinful nature, from that nature will reap destruction; the one who sows to please the Spirit, from the Spirit will reap eternal life."

The effects of karma may be experienced in the present life or in the next life. Meritorious or "good" acts may mean rebirth into a high level, such as a superior human or a godlike being, while evil acts result in rebirth as a human living in miserable circumstances or as a lower animal.

How do we escape the law of karma and the endless cycle of birth, death, and rebirth? Karma is rooted in the five afflictions (i.e., the klesas), and as long as the klesas remain, reincarnation is the inevitable result. Swami Rajarshi Muni explains this process as follows:

These klesas are responsible not only for the embodiment or the bondage of the soul but also for its status and condition in the present life, depending upon the merits and the demerits acquired by it during the past lives. They impair pure consciousness and weaken the mind. So long as the roots exist, a tree grows and bears fruit. Similarly, the latent karmas bear fruit as long as their roots in the form of klesas exist. The yogis annihilate the latent karmas by way of removing their foundation, the klesas. Just as a burnt seed cannot germinate, so also the burnt seeds of the latent karmas cannot sprout.

The goal of Kriya Yoga is to eliminate the klesas so that we may ultimately reach samadhi. This occurs only when a state of discriminative discernment—viveka—is reached. Briefly, when we are in this state, we understand the difference between our everyday minds and the true Self. The klesas are destroyed, and all of the seeds of karma are burned away. The cycle of samsara ends, our actions produce no more karma, and we are united with our true Self.

Karma has roots in the five afflictions which may come to fruition in present or future lives.
Klesa mulah karma asayo drsta adrsta janma vedaniyah

Thus, the most important purpose and reason of rebirth is to attain liberation, to become one with God. People can go astray in one life. Yet God wants us all to come to Him. That is the purpose of human birth. So, He gives us more chances. We keep coming back until we learn the lessons of this human birth and until we transcend the limitations and temptations of the flesh. Thus, we must realize that everything we do which is not conducive to the path of God realization is simply an obstacle we are putting in our own way. It is simply one more hurdle we will have to cross, if not this life then the next life.

H. H. Sri Pujya Swami Chidanand Saraswatiji

As long as the roots (of affliction)
remain, karma produces
three consequences: form of birth, span of
life, and life experiences.

Sati mule tad vipako jaty ayur bhogah

The roots, the causes, the Samskaras (i.e., the store-house of karmas) being there, they again manifest and form the effects. The cause becomes the effect, and the effect becomes more subtle and becomes the cause of the next effect. The tree bears a seed and becomes the cause of the next tree, and so on. All our works now are the effects of past Samskaras. Again, these Samskaras become the cause of future actions, and thus we go on.

Sri Swami Vivekananda

Because of virtue or vice these three (birth, span of life, and life experiences) may produce pleasure or pain.
Te hlada paritapa phalah punya
apunya hetutvat

The king said: Why is it, Nâgasena, that all men are not alike, but some are short-lived and some long-lived, some sickly and some healthy, some ugly and some beautiful, some without influence and some of great power, some poor and some wealthy, some low born and some high born, some stupid and some wise?'

The Elder replied: "Why is it that all vegetables are not alike, but some sour, and some salt, and some pungent, and some acid, and some astringent, and some sweet?"

"I fancy, Sir, it is because they come from different kinds of seeds."

King Milinda

The Cause of Suffering

The disunited mind is far from wise; how can it meditate? How be at peace? When you know no peace, how can you know joy? When you let your mind follow the call of the senses, they carry away your better judgment as storms drive a boat off its charted course on the sea. Use all your power to free the senses from attachment and aversion alike, and live in the full wisdom of the Self.

Bhagavad Gita, Chapter Two, Verses 66–68

The yogis say that the man who has discriminating powers, the man of good sense, sees through all things which are called pleasure and pain and knows that they are always equally distributed, and that one follows the other and melts into the other; he sees that men are following an ignis fatuus (i.e., an illusory light) all their lives and never succeed in fulfilling their desires. There was never a love in this world which did not know decay.

Sri Swami Vivekananda

Upon a first reading, Sutra 2.15 appears to adopt a pessimistic and defeatist view toward life. Is it really true that all experiences inherently contain the seeds of suffering? If so, are we condemned to a life of suffering and misery? Is suffering always contained within such beautiful experiences as love, success, beauty, nature, and art?

This sutra points to a great truth in the wisdom traditions. A person who has attained wisdom through spiritual practice understands that all everyday experiences ultimately lead to suffering. This sutra describes the inner workings of suffering and is similar to the first two truths of the Buddha's Four Noble Truths. The Four Noble Truths state that life is full of suffering, that there is a cause of suffering, a way to end suffering, and that the way is the Noble Eightfold Path.

Patanjali gives us four reasons why all experiences lead to suffering. These are based on the notion that suffering is built into the very fabric of our everyday experiences.

The first reason is change (*parinama*). It is obvious that life is impermanent and is in a perpetual state of change. We can see change in the birth, life, and death of the stars and galaxies in the universe, the constant geological forces acting on our own planet, the state of our own bodies, the activity in our minds, as well as our relationships and in our physical possessions. Nothing is permanent, nothing is fixed, nothing is immutable. All evolve, grow, shrink, decay, change; no state is steady. We suffer because we crave permanence. We want to keep what we have, we want perfect moments to continue forever, we want the security that is born of permanence, and we do not want to face difficult situations that arise through time, change, or other forces beyond our control. It is the conflict between our natural, innate psychological desire for security and permanence, and the inevitable fact of impermanence that creates suffering.

The second reason we suffer is anxiety (*tapa*). This refers to a latent feeling that we will inevitably lose those things to which we are attached and that our feeling of security and sense of well-being will be threatened. This anxiety can range from relationships, to material possessions, job-security, personal health, and existential worry. We know in our heart of hearts that we are really not secure and that our castles are built on sand.

The third reason we suffer comes from the actions of subliminal impressions (*samskaras*). Samskara refers to habits. Like the needle cutting a grove in a record, we acquire habits or patterns based upon our life experiences. But the world often forces us to break our habits, and the result is anxiety, worry, and suffering as we are forced to try new things, to change or to do things outside of our comfort zone. Our habits may also be negative or self-destructive and thereby create more suffering.

The fourth reason is the activity of the *gunas*. The gunas will be treated more fully in the next block of sutras. They are the primal forces that create all of the elements that comprise the natural world, including our bodies and minds. The gunas are *rajas* (activity, passion), *tamas* (heaviness, dullness), and *sattva* (light, clarity). The gunas are in a constant state of flux and imbalance; it is as if they are in an eternal dance in which each strives to take the lead. Because the gunas directly affect our mental states, our minds tend to be in constant motion and change. This is where the idea of the "monkey mind" comes from!

Sometimes we feel heavy, lethargic and uninspired, other times we are full of energy and activity, and at still other times we are happy and full of lightness. We may even feel combinations of these three qualities. This is all the result of the gunas acting on our minds. Because the gunas cause change and exert a powerful force on our minds, we often feel unstable and anxious. We crave permanence, stability, and security, but the gunas are too powerful for us to control.

These forces cause suffering in our daily lives. We may feel that we are trapped by life. We may feel that we don't get what we want and get what we don't want. We want permanence, but we know it is not to be. Are we eternally chained to these forces and condemned to lives of suffering, or is there a way out?

Patanjali gives us good news. There is a way to rise and conquer these forces and end our suffering. As we will see in the following sutras, we can end suffering through the discernment and right knowledge we obtain from the practice of Yoga.

The wise know that everything leads
to suffering because of impermanence,
the suffering caused by pain itself, and
the mental impressions (samskaras) and
fluctuations (vrittis). All are caused by the
qualities of nature (the gunas).

Parinama tapa samskara duhkhair
guna vrtti virodhac ca duhkham eva
sarvam vivekinah

Here, Patanjali gives a very important Sutra and a great
truth in the spiritual field. If we could only contemplate
this for at least a little while daily, our lives would be
completely transformed. All experiences are painful for
the person of spiritual discrimination. In this world, all
experiences that come from outside through the world,
through nature or material things, are ultimately painful.
None can give everlasting happiness. They may give
temporary pleasure, but they always end in pain. Even
the enjoyment of present pleasures is usually painful
because we fear its loss.

Sri Swami Satchidananda

Suffering that has yet to come should be avoided.

Heyam duhkham anagatam

The Buddha said, "I only teach two things: I teach about suffering and the way out of suffering." Your time should be devoted to the study and the practice of these two things. And when we are able to liberate ourselves from suffering our mind becomes clear; then our mind can reflect ultimate reality without any intellectual searching. Your mind will become like a mirror that can reflect reality as it is, without any distortion.

Thich Nhat Hanh

Purusha, Prakriti, and the Gunas: Samkhya Philosophy

Like two golden birds perched
on the selfsame tree,
intimate friends, the ego and the Self
dwell in the same body.
The former eats the sweet and sour fruits
of the tree of life,
while the latter looks on with detachment.
As long as we think we are the ego,
we feel attached and fall into sorrow.
But realize that you are the Self, the Lord of life,
and you will be freed from sorrow.

The Mundaka Upanishad, Chapter 3, Verses 1–3

Ignorance exists as long as the illusion of the world is not
completely forgotten.

Baba Hari Dass

The Indian wisdom tradition recognizes six *darshanas* or classical schools of philosophy. These schools grew out of the ancient teachings received by the divinely inspired rishis (sages), which were later embodied in the Vedas and the Upanishads. All of the darshanas may be viewed as complementary disciplines, as if they are branches of a single tree. The darshanas are often related in pairs of two. Yoga and Samkhya are often viewed as a complementary pair. The Yoga Sutras are built on Samkhya philosophy. The principles of Purusha, Prakriti, and the gunas all come from Samkhya.

The term *Samkhya* is derived from the Sanskrit word meaning "exact knowing." Samkhya is concerned with the evolutionary process by which the universe unfolds from subtle energies through twenty-five categories of very subtle to progressively grosser matter. Yoga Sutras 2.17-2.24 discuss Samkhya philosophy.

In the Samkhya system, there are two fundamental principles: *Purusha* and *Prakriti*. Purusha is the true Self. It is spirit. It is the male principle, and its nature is static, eternal, and unchanging. It is pure consciousness, and it is beyond words or form. Purusha does not act. Its role is to observe the eternal dance of the universe as a spectator. Purusha manifests in each one of us as the true Self, the Seer or the Witness.

Prakriti is the natural world. It is the energy that is the prime mover of creation, out of which the world is born and into which it is dissolved. It is the female principle. Prakriti is the elements, the mind and the other sense organs. Prakriti includes the entire cosmos-the formless energy field, the physical forms of nature, and the psychological processes of the mind. Prakriti is everything that has name and form. It is mind, energy, and matter.

Prakriti has three qualities, which are known as the gunas. The gunas, again, are rajas (activity, passion), tamas (heaviness, dullness), and sattva (light, clarity). They underlie all physical, psychological, and moral realities.

When the gunas are in a state of balance, Prakriti resides in a still and formless state. Nothing exists. However, when this state of balance is disrupted by the presence of Purusha's pure awareness, the process of the manifestation of the universe begins to unfold, and it evolves into the perpetually changing forms of nature. The vast and complex interplay of the gunas creates the five elements (earth, water, fire, air, and ether) and the entire structure of the universe. Purusha remains passive, undisturbed, and formless during the process of Prakriti's creation of the universe.

As we saw in Sutra 2.15, the gunas are responsible for human suffering because they cause our minds to be unstable and to change constantly. Because we naturally identify with our everyday mind, we lose sight of our true Self, or Purusha. This false identification with our everyday mind and all of its instability, conflicts and anxieties—rather than with our true Self- causes suffering.

There are two key points that should be understood from Sutras 2.17-2.24. The first relates to the cause of suffering. Sutra 2.17 teaches that suffering is caused by the association of Purusha and Prakriti. Our everyday mind and senses pull Purusha outward into the world of Prakriti, and Purusha mistakenly identifies with the manifestations of Prakriti. Thus, we imagine that we are happy, unhappy, angry, or peaceful.

Liberation from suffering occurs when Purusha and Prakriti are separated and Purusha rests in its true Self. Professor Ian Whicher explains this as follows: "Paradoxically, it appears that purusha is both aware of its transcendent nature as the 'seer' (Yoga Sutra 1.3), and yet it is seemingly and mysteriously 'entrapped' in prakriti whereby human identity experiences itself to be a finite entity through a process of 'conformity' (*sarupya*, Yoga Sutra 1.4) to the nature of the modifications (*vrtti*) of the mind *(citta).*"

Our consciousness is a result of the association between the pure consciousness of Purusha and the everyday mind that is Prakriti. However, even though Purusha associates with Prakriti, its essential nature remains unchanged. This has been expressed by comparing the mind to a crystal that reflects the color of an object near it, while its clarity remains unchanged.

But why does this association of Purusha with Prakriti cause suffering? Sri Swami Satchidananda explains this in a simple and beautiful way:

The Purusha is the true Self. It is the Purusha who sees. The Prakriti is everything else. All other things beside you are the seen. But it seems we always identify ourselves with what is seen, with what we possess. . . This identification with other things is the cause of all of our pain. Instead if we are just ourselves always, things may change or stay as they are, but they will never cause us pain because the changes will be in the things we possess and not in us.

It is our Purusha that we seek to liberate from its entanglement with the manifestations of Prakriti. As we have seen in Sutra 1.3, if we can end the misidentification with the modifications of our minds, then we can abide in our true Self (Purusha).

The second key point is that our false identification with Prakriti is caused by avidya (spiritual ignorance). However, through the practice of Yoga, we may acquire the wisdom that overcomes our ignorance about our true Self (our Purusha). This wisdom is known as viveka, and it is a state of profound discrimination and right knowledge. We will explore viveka in the next group of sutras.

The cause of suffering is the identification of the seer (Purusha) with that which is seen (Prakriti) and should be avoided.

Drastr drsyayoh samyoga heya hetuh

Who is the seer? The Self of Man, the Purusha. What is the seen? The whole of nature, beginning with the mind, down to gross matter. All this pleasure and pain arises from the junction between this Purusha and the mind. The Purusha, you must remember, according to this philosophy, is pure; it is when it is joined to nature, and by reflection, that it appears to feel either pleasure or pain.

Sri Swami Vivekananda

**The seen (Prakriti) consists of
the senses and the elements.
Its nature is illumination
(sattva), activity (rajas), and inertia
(tamas). Its purpose is to provide
experience and to liberate Purusha.**
Prakasa kriya sthiti silam bhuta indriya
atmakam bhoga apavarga
artham drsyam

*The "seen" is nature or Prakriti (from the verb root, kr,
"to make or do," and, pra, "to bring forth"). For the yogi,
each and every event, whether marvelous or difficult to
bear, is filled with meaning. Everything that happens is
for the purpose of giving experiences to the Purusha. Or,
more correctly, the experiences are for the mind, since
the Purusha is by nature free. All Yoga theories and
practices are for the sake of liberating the individual
from the limitations of the ego and obscuring the power
of ignorance. The "experiences" mentioned in this sutra
are learning experiences. They are the spiritual lessons
that help turn our attention to the Self.*

Reverend Jaganath Carrera

The gunas have four stages.
These are the defined, the undefined, the specific, and the non-specific.

Visesa avisesa linga matra alingani
guna parvani

The claim of the Sankhya philosophy is that beginning with the intellect and coming down to a block of stone, all has come out of the same thing, only as finer or grosser states of existence.

Now we shall understand the aphorism, that the states of the qualities are defined, undefined, and signless. By the defined is meant the gross elements, which we can sense. By the undefined is meant the very fine materials, the Tanmatras, which cannot be sensed by ordinary men. If you practice Yoga, however, says Patanjali, after a while your perception will become so fine that you will actually see the Tanmatras.

Sri Swami Vivekananda

The Seer (Purusha) is only the power of seeing. Although it is pure, the Seer witnesses the images of the mind.

Drasta drsi matrah suddha api
pratyaya anupasyah

I know the great Purusha, who is luminous like the sun and beyond darkness. Only by knowing Him does one pass over death; there is no other way to the Supreme Goal. The whole universe is filled by Purusha, to whom there is nothing superior, from whom there is nothing different, from whom there is nothing either smaller or greater; who stands alone, motionless as a tree, established in His own glory.

Svetasvatara Upanishad Chapter 3, Verses 8-10, 12

The nature of the seen (Prakriti) is to exist only for the sake of the Seer (Purusha).

Tad artha eva drsyasya atma

Nature has no light of its own. As long as the Purusha is present in it, it appears light, but the light is borrowed, just as the moon's light is reflected. All the manifestations of nature are caused by this nature itself, according to the Yogis, but nature has no purpose in view, except to free the Purusa.

Sri Swami Vivekananda

Although the seen (Prakriti) ceases
to exist for those who have attained
liberation (its purpose having
been fulfilled), it continues
for others since it is a
common experience of all
other beings.

Krta artham prati nastam apy anastam tad
anya sadha ranatvat

*The Purusha is, says the Gita, witness, upholder,
source of the sanction, knower, lord, enjoyer; Prakriti
executes, it is the active principle and must have
an operation corresponding to the attitude of the
Purusha. The soul may assume, if it wishes, the
poise of the pure witness; it may look on at the
action of Nature as a thing from which it stands
apart; it watches, but does not itself participate . . .
It is the basis of the movement of withdrawal by
which we can say of everything. This is Prakriti
working in the life, mind and body; it is not myself;
it is not even mine.*

Sri Aurobindo

The union of Purusha and Prakriti causes the recognition of both of their natures and powers.

Sva svami saktyoh sva rupa upalabdhi
hetuh samyogah

Know that prakriti and Purusha are both without beginning, and that from prakriti come the gunas and all that changes. Prakriti is the agent, cause and effect of every action, but it is Purusha that seems to experience pleasure and pain.

Purusha, resting in prakriti, witnesses the play of the gunas born of prakriti.

But attachment to the gunas leads a person to be born good or evil.

Within the body, the supreme Purusha is called the witness, approver, supporter, enjoyer, the supreme Lord, the highest Self. Whoever realizes the true nature of Purusha, prakriti, and the gunas, whatever path he or she may follow, is not born separate again.

The Bhagavad Gita, Chapter 13, Verses 19–23

Spiritual ignorance is the cause of the false union of the seer (Purusha) with the seen (Prakriti).

Tasya hetuh avidya

The "experiencer" is the Atman, our real nature. The "object of experience" is the totality of the apparent world, including the mind and the senses. In reality, the Atman alone exists, "One without a second," eternally free. But by the false identification through maya, which is the mystery of our present predicament, the Atman is mistaken for the individual ego, subject to all the thought-waves which arise and trouble the mind. That is why we imagine that we are "unhappy" or "happy", "angry" or "lustful."

Christopher Isherwood

Escape from Suffering: Viveka

This is the real goal of practice, discrimination between the real and unreal, knowing that the Purusha is not nature, that it is neither matter nor mind, and that because it is not nature, it cannot possibly change. It is only nature which changes, combining and recombining, dissolving continually. When through constant practice we begin to discriminate, ignorance will vanish, and the Purusha will begin to shine in its real nature, omniscient, omnipotent, omnipresent.

Sri Swami Vivekenanda

Spiritual ignorance (avidya) is the cause of suffering. If we can remove spiritual ignorance, we can end suffering. Viveka is the ability to liberate ourselves from ignorance and to discriminate between our true Self and our identification with our ordinary thoughts and experiences, which we mistakenly believe to be our true identity. Thus, viveka is one of the keys to the entire science of Yoga. In Sutra 2.28, Patanjali teaches that we achieve viveka through the practice of the eight limbs of Yoga. Through this practice, impurities are removed, wisdom emerges, and the state of viveka is realized. Reverend Jaganath Carrera explains as follows:

Ordinarily our discriminative capacity is occupied with a constant stream of pertinent and nonpertinent thoughts: perceptions of objects, events, wishes, and people flow into that consciousness. But to pierce through ignorance, to perceive the Self as our true identity, viveka requires a high order of clear, steady focus and the absence of selfish attachment.

As we saw in our discussion in the Introduction to Sutras 2.17–2.24, as a result of spiritual ignorance, Purusha loses sight of its true nature as pure awareness and becomes identified with Prakriti. Because Prakriti is impermanent and is perpetually changing, suffering is the result. However, when the discrimination born of the light of wisdom is realized, Purusha withdraws from its entanglement with Prakriti and rests in its pure awareness. Because we have realized our true Self (as Purusha), our suffering ends, and we become liberated beings.

The removal of ignorance ends the union of the Seer (Purusha) and the seen (Prakriti). This is the liberation of the Seer.
Tad abhavat samyoga abhavo hanam
tad drseh kaivalyam

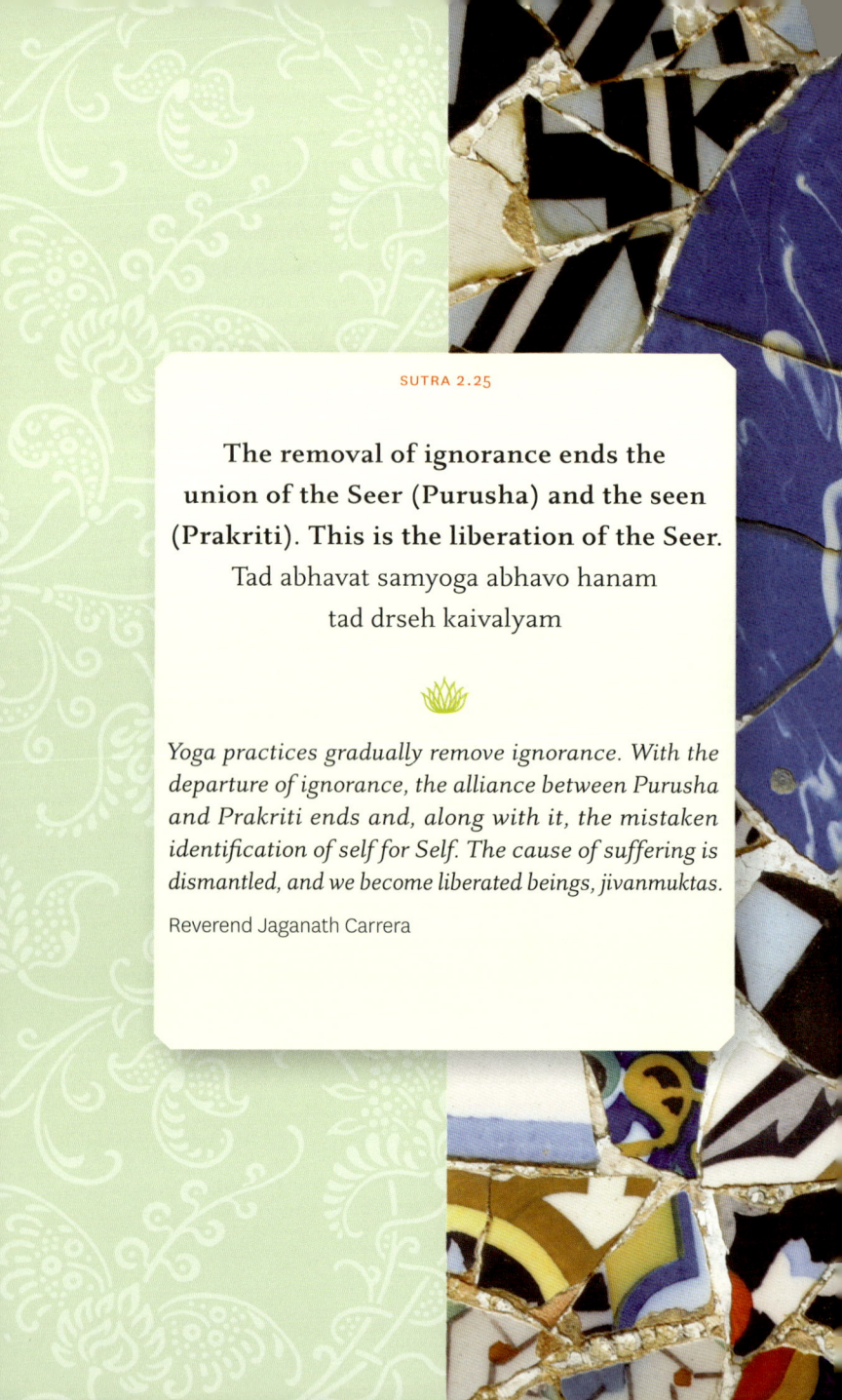

Yoga practices gradually remove ignorance. With the departure of ignorance, the alliance between Purusha and Prakriti ends and, along with it, the mistaken identification of self for Self. The cause of suffering is dismantled, and we become liberated beings, jivanmuktas.

Reverend Jaganath Carrera

The uninterrupted practice of discriminative knowledge (viveka) is the means to liberation.

Viveka khyatir aviplava hana upayah

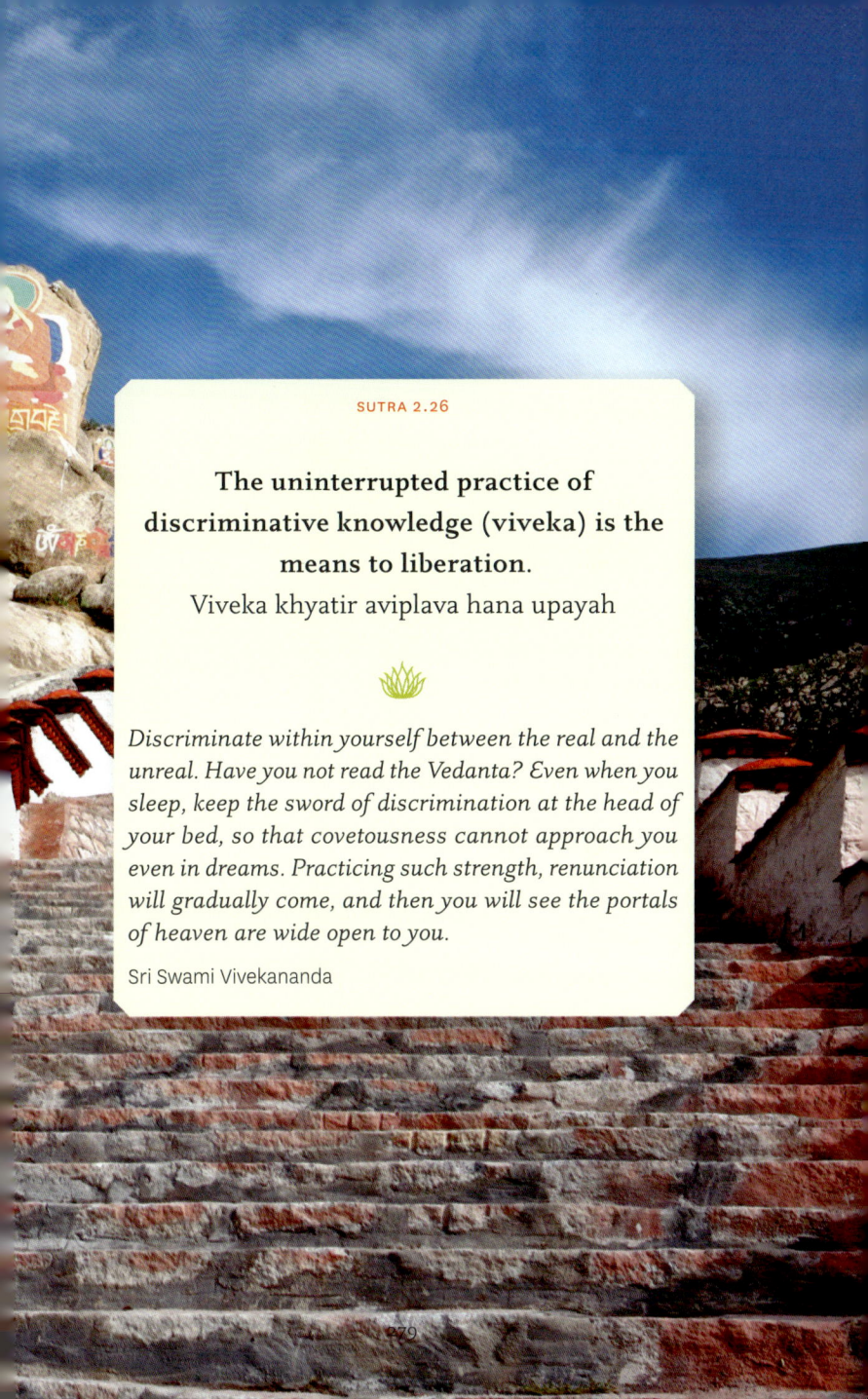

Discriminate within yourself between the real and the unreal. Have you not read the Vedanta? Even when you sleep, keep the sword of discrimination at the head of your bed, so that covetousness cannot approach you even in dreams. Practicing such strength, renunciation will gradually come, and then you will see the portals of heaven are wide open to you.

Sri Swami Vivekananda

The highest wisdom
has seven stages.
Tasya saptadha pranta bhumih prajna

I thought that my voyage had come to its end
at the last limit of my power—
that the path before me was closed,
that provisions were exhausted,
and the time come to take shelter in
a silent obscurity.
But I find that thy will knows no end in me.
And when old words die out on the tongue,
new melodies break forth from the heart,
and where the old tracks are lost,
new country is revealed with its wonders.

Rabindranath Tagore

The Eightfold Path of Yoga

In his compendium of wisdom, inspiration, and insight titled the Yoga Sutras Patanjali explains yoga as an eight-limbed tree, with the highest branch being Samadhi, or the ultimate, divine bliss and ecstasy, which comes from complete, transcendental union with the Divine. The foundation of the tree are the yamas and the niyamas (the moral and ethical code of conduct), and one moves upward through asana and pranayama, which use the body and the breath as the medium, then into the aspects in which one's mind becomes fine-tuned and ultimately united with God, and ultimately to the state of divine liberation.

But when I say you will attain liberation, I am not talking about only an abstract and vague concept in which after death you merge into Oneness with the Divine. No. I am talking about liberation here on Earth. Liberation while living. Liberation every moment of every day. What is that liberation? It is liberation from anger. Liberation from greed. Liberation from worry. Liberation from desires. Liberation from despair. Liberation from depression.

H. H. Pujya Swami Chidanand Saraswatiji

In Sutra 2.28, Patanjali elegantly describes the results of practicing Yoga in a single sutra. Through the devoted practice of Yoga, our moral, physical, and mental impurities are cleansed, true wisdom (viveka) is acquired, and the klesas (including spiritual ignorance) are destroyed. The ultimate goal of Yoga—to end the misidentification with the fluctuations of our minds so that we may reside in our true Self—is reached.

Patanjali established the eight limbed path which is commonly known as Astanga Yoga. This path is yama (restraints), niyama (observances), asana (posture), pranayama (breath control), pratyahara (sense withdrawal), dharana (concentration), dhyana (meditation), and samadhi (absorption). It is comprised of both an external and an internal journey.

The external journey involves the first five practices—yama, niyama, asana, pranayama, and pratyahara. These are considered external because they relate to the body and our relationship with the external world. The remaining sutras in Pada 2 address these practices. When we have mastered the external practices, we are ready for the internal journey.

The internal journey is the last three practices: dharana, dhyana, and samadhi. They are known as *samyama*. They are more fully explored in Sutras 3.4 and 3.5. These practices are considered internal because they involve expanding consciousness. The purpose of progressing through the three stages of samyama is to develop the light of wisdom so that we can discriminate between Purusha and Prakriti. In this state, spiritual ignorance (avidya) is ended. This deep process leads to the realization that Purusha, the true Self, is the core of our being.

By the dedicated practice
of the limbs of Yoga, the impurities
are destroyed, the light of wisdom
dawns, and discriminative
discernment is realized.

Yoga anga anusthanad asuddhi ksaye
jnana diptir a viveka khyateh

If you work on yoga, yoga will work on you.

Baba Hari Dass

The eight limbs of yoga are yama, niyama, asana, pranayama, pratyahara, dharana, dhyana, and samadhi.

Yama niyama asana pranayama
pratyahara dharana dhyana samadhayo
stav angani

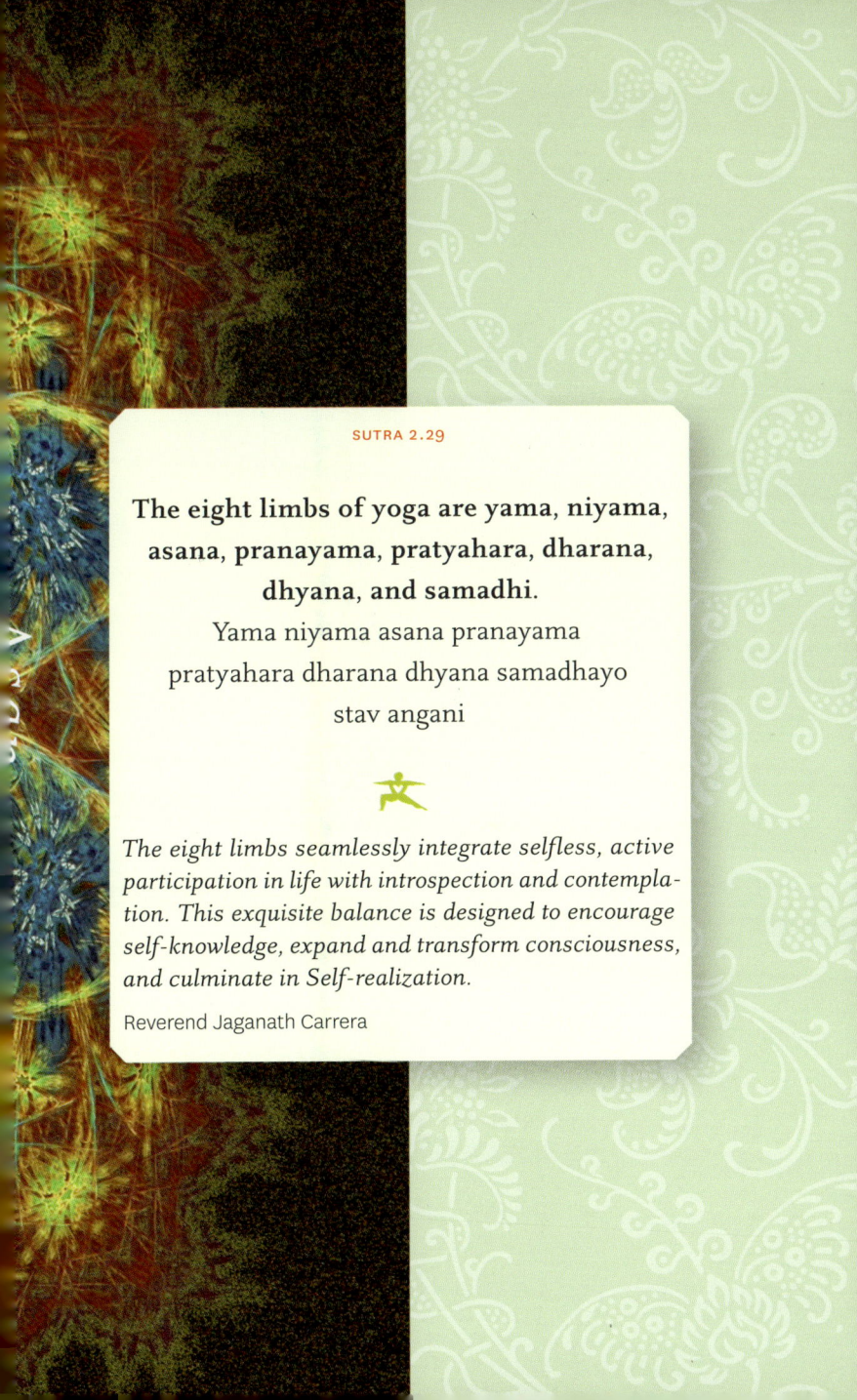

The eight limbs seamlessly integrate selfless, active participation in life with introspection and contemplation. This exquisite balance is designed to encourage self-knowledge, expand and transform consciousness, and culminate in Self-realization.

Reverend Jaganath Carrera

Restraints and Observances— Yamas, Niyamas and Pratipaksa

The Yamas and Niyamas are the beginnings, which really last till the end of Yoga. Even as education in the primary school level is important, since it paves the way for one's further mental build, the Yamas and Niyamas are the rock bottom of Yoga. The student enters the practical field of meditation after being built up by the tonic of Yamas and Niyamas, which provide the power and courage needed to face all obstacles. Meditation is not difficult to achieve if the necessary preparations are made earlier. The Yama-Niyama process constitutes the instructions in yoga psychology, which should give us sufficient warning on the path and make us vigilant pilgrims on the spiritual journey.

Sri Swami Krishnananda

The yamas and niyamas provide a solid moral foundation for the practice of Yoga. The yamas are *ahimsa* (non-violence), *satya* (truthfulness), *asteya* (non-stealing), *brahmacarya* (moderation), and *aparigraha* (non-greed). The yamas guide our actions, speech and thought in the external world. They are sometimes referred to as the great vows. Patanjali taught that these are absolute vows that we must follow without excuses or exceptions.

The niyamas are *saucha* (bodily purity), *santosha* (contentment), *tapas* (austerities), *svadhyaya* (self or spiritual study), and *Isvara pranidhanani* (devotion to God). The niyamas are practices that involve self-discipline. The yamas and niyamas prepare us to successfully practice Yoga by providing us with a healthy body, clear mind, and regulated senses.

The concept of *pratipaksa* (i.e., the opposite direction or thought) is introduced in Sutras 2.33 and 2.34. By practicing pratipaksa, we learn to counterbalance our thoughts and actions that may violate the yamas and the niyamas. Swami Jnaneshvara Bharati explains pratipaksa as follows:

What does opposite direction mean? When thinking of anger or hatred, for example, it can seem that one should cultivate love, which is a good idea. However, you may have noticed how hard it is to cultivate love for one with whom you are intensely angry. The word opposite is used here to suggest that rather than going into or getting caught up in that anger, we move away from it, in the opposite direction, which is not quite the same as saying we should cultivate love. Recall the foundation principle that consciousness wraps itself around the thought patterns in the mind field, and that this is the cause of suffering. When we unwrap our attention from those thought patterns, we rest in our true nature. This is the meaning of moving in the

opposite direction; it means moving away from the entanglement of the negative. By moving away, we naturally experience the love.

I have found this to be a very helpful sutra to use in dealing with difficult people. We all have had experiences with certain people who have the ability to get under our skin and whose very presence in the room seems to throw us off balance and produce feelings of defensiveness, hostility, or resentment. If we are in a situation where we cannot escape being around such a person, perhaps at work or in a relationship, we are presented with conflicts between this person and the feelings they generate in our minds. We build walls, engage in endless internal dialogues about the person, express the conflict in anger, aggressiveness, or withdrawal, or seek to repress the conflict. The tendency is to get stuck in a cycle that never reaches a resolution and seems to intensify over time.

Let's consider the use of pratipaksa in this situation. First, we should remind ourselves that this mental cycle is not useful and will bring nothing but more suffering. We need to change our response to the situation.

We can cultivate an opposing emotion, feeling, or energy. Why not visualize approaching this person with mental images of kindness, compassion, and peace? Why not imagine a positive interaction or a successful conversation? By using pratipaksa we can change the dynamic of the entire situation. By projecting positive energies, we may find that the person returns the positive energy. It is like using baking soda to take the sting out of an insect bite. Since baking soda is an alkaline, it neutralizes the acid in the poison.

**The great universal vows (the yamas)
are non-violence, truthfulness,
non-stealing, moderation,
and non-greed.**
Ahimsa satya asteya brahmacarya
aparigraha yamah

*Yoga is search for Truth in its ultimate reaches and
above its relative utility. Adequate preparations have to
be made for this adventure. We have to become honest
before Truth, and not merely in the eyes of our friends.
This openness before the Absolute is the meaning behind
the observance of what Yoga calls Yamas, as a course
of self-discipline which one imposes upon oneself for
attaining that moral nature consistent with the demands
of Truth . . . Any conduct which cannot be in harmony
with the universal cannot ultimately be moral, at least
in the sense Yoga requires it.*

Sri Swami Krishnananda

The yamas are the great universal vows. They are not limited by place, time, or class.

Jati desa kala samaya anavacchinnah
sarva bhauma maha vratam

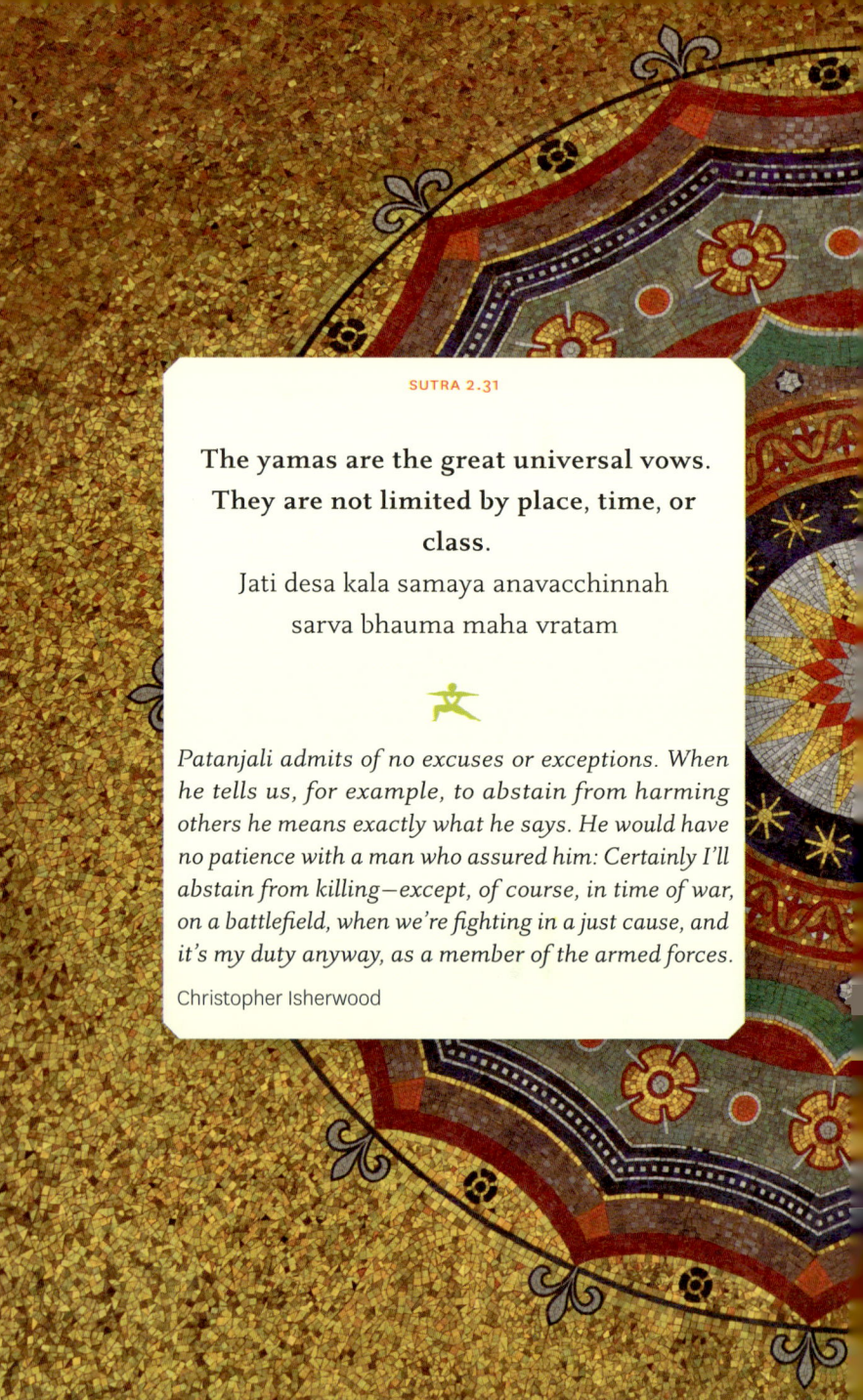

Patanjali admits of no excuses or exceptions. When he tells us, for example, to abstain from harming others he means exactly what he says. He would have no patience with a man who assured him: Certainly I'll abstain from killing—except, of course, in time of war, on a battlefield, when we're fighting in a just cause, and it's my duty anyway, as a member of the armed forces.

Christopher Isherwood

**The observances (the niyamas) are purity,
contentment, austerity,
study of spiritual texts, and devotion to
Isvara
(the Supreme Being).**
Sauca santosha tapah svadhyaya isvara
pranidhanani niyamah

*Once we have mastered our bodies and minds through
the spiritual and ethical observances of the yamas,
we will move to a higher spiritual path. Thereafter, we
have the five niyamas. In Sanskrit, the word "niyama"
means a rule or a law or a standard practice. These
five niyamas are internal laws, rules which we set for
ourselves, to which we adhere in our quest for a disciplined, yogic life.*

H. H. Pujya Swami Chidanand Saraswatiji

When disturbed by negative thoughts, one should cultivate positive thoughts.

Vitarka badhane pratipaksa
bhavanam

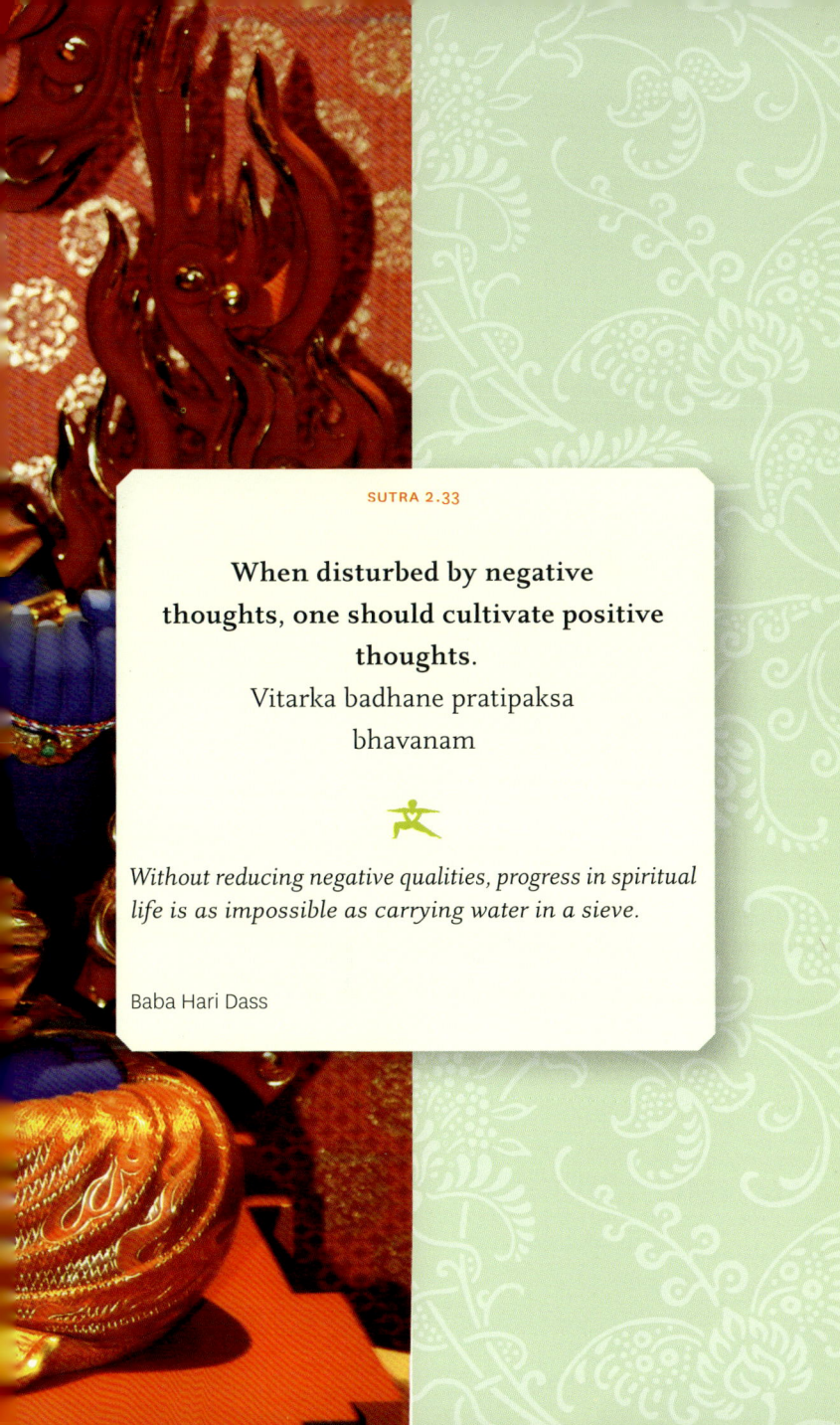

Without reducing negative qualities, progress in spiritual life is as impossible as carrying water in a sieve.

Baba Hari Dass

Actions performed out of negative thoughts (such as violence, greed, anger, or delusion) are contrary to Yoga. These may be mild, moderate, or intense and result in suffering. This is true even if they are performed by oneself, on one's behalf by another, or by another person with approval. Reflecting on their opposites will end suffering.

Vitarka himsa adayah krta karita
anumodita lobha krodha moha purvaka
mrdu madhya adhimatra
duhkha ajnana ananta phala iti
pratipaksa bhavanam

How are these fine Samskaras to be controlled? We have to begin with the big waves, and come down and down. For instance, when a big wave of anger has come into the mind, how are we to control that? Just by raising a big opposing wave. Think of love. Sometimes a mother is very angry with her husband, and while in that state the baby comes in, and she kisses the baby; the old wave dies out, and a new wave arises, love for the child. That suppresses the other one. Love is opposite to anger. So we find that by raising the opposite waves we can conquer those which we want to reject. Then, if we can raise in our fine nature those fine opposing waves, they will check the fine workings of anger beneath the conscious surface.

Sri Swami Vivekananda

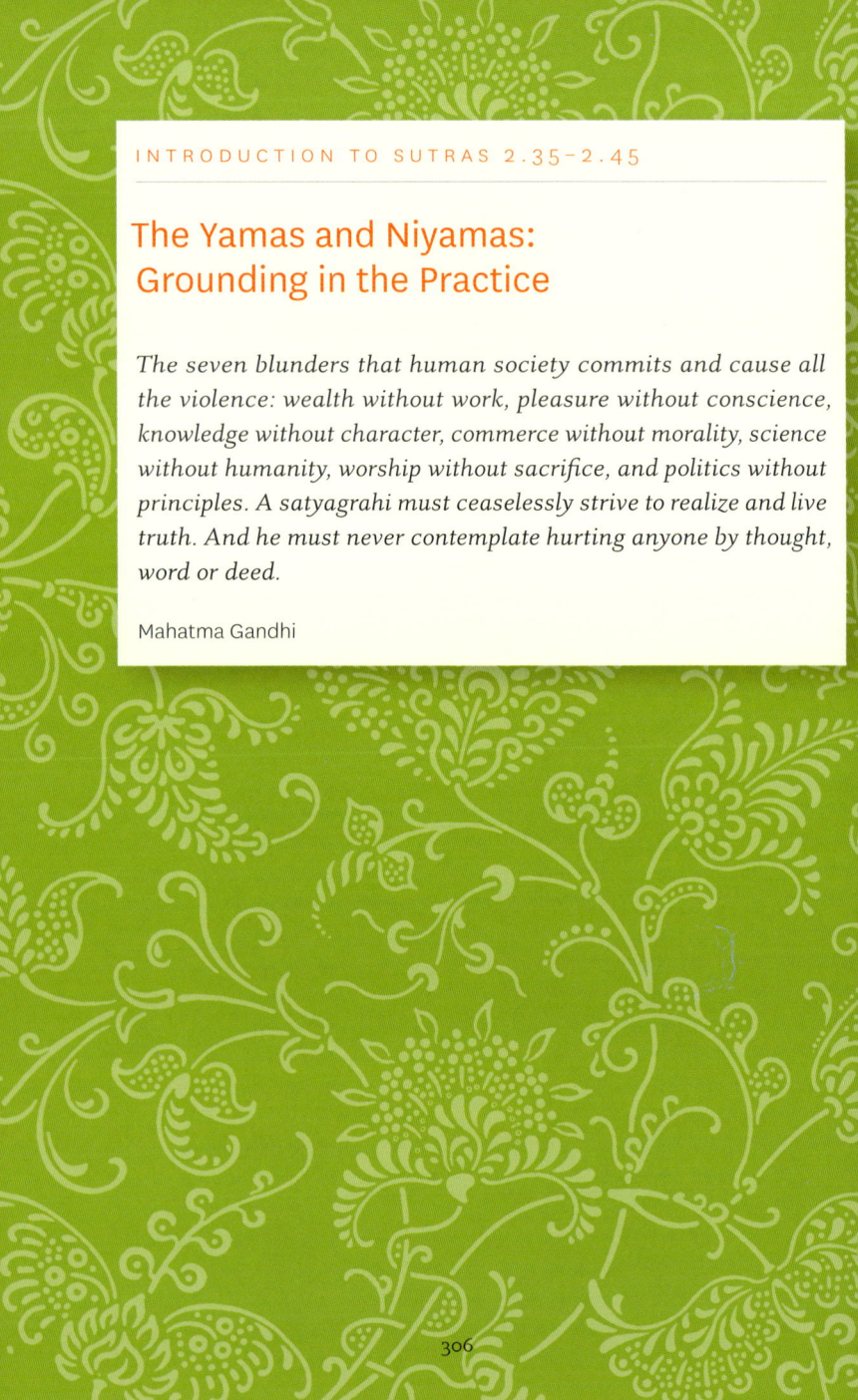

The Yamas and Niyamas: Grounding in the Practice

The seven blunders that human society commits and cause all the violence: wealth without work, pleasure without conscience, knowledge without character, commerce without morality, science without humanity, worship without sacrifice, and politics without principles. A satyagrahi must ceaselessly strive to realize and live truth. And he must never contemplate hurting anyone by thought, word or deed.

Mahatma Gandhi

Our spiritual life in Yoga is built upon the moral code embodied in the yamas and niyamas, and they establish the foundation of our practice as we follow the eight-limbed path. This moral code is similar to those in other wisdom traditions. For example, the five yamas and the five niyamas suggest the Ten Commandments of the Jewish and Christian traditions, as well as the ten virtues of Buddhism.

The yamas are known as the great moral vows. In Sutra 2.31, Patanjali teaches us that these vows are universal and are not limited by class, place, or time. They are our guiding principles regardless of our situation, our culture, or our status in life.

All of us have been in situations where we face the dilemma of whether to follow a moral vow or make an exception due to special circumstances. Should we tell a white lie to avoid hurting the feelings of another person? Should we steal food to feed ourselves or our children if we have no money? Should we commit a violent act to prevent greater harm to another?

Patanjali makes it clear that there are no exceptions to the yamas; that they may not be broken under any circumstances. He sets an extraordinarily high standard of conduct for us to meet, and we should be prepared to follow the right path even though we anticipate it may be difficult. Sri Swami Krishnananda observed that:

To be moral is to establish a concord between our own nature and the nature of that which we seek in life. Yoga is our interview with the Supreme Being, and here our nature corresponds to its highest reaches.

The niyamas are the personal observances. In contrast to the yamas, which regulate social life, the niyamas are concerned with one's personal discipline and practice. The yamas are directed at establishing a strong moral and ethical foundation for yogic life, whereas the niyamas are concerned with preparing the way for the discipline that is necessary to follow the eight-limbed path.

AHIMSA SUTRA 2.35

In the presence of one who is established in non-violence, all hostility ends.
Ahimsa pratisthayam tat samnidhau
vaira tyagah

This is the fundamental, most basic, and crucial tenet of living as a good human. Do not cause pain or injury to another. However, ahimsa does not pertain only to our physical actions. It does not simply mean "Thou shall not kill" or "Thou shall not hit." Rather it encompasses all forms of violence—violence in thought, violence in speech, and violence in deed. We must think pure and loving thoughts. We must speak pure and loving words, and we must practice pure and loving acts.

H. H. Pujya Swami Chidanand Saraswatiji

When one is firmly established in truthfulness, the fruits of action are obtained.

Satya pratisthayam kriya phala asrayatvam

An ordinary man is said to be truthful when his words correspond to the facts of which he speaks. But when a man becomes perfected in truthfulness, he gains control, so to speak, of the truth. He no longer has to "obey" facts; facts obey him. He cannot think or even dream a lie; everything he says becomes true. If he blesses someone, that person is blessed—no matter whether the blessing was deserved or not.

Christopher Isherwood

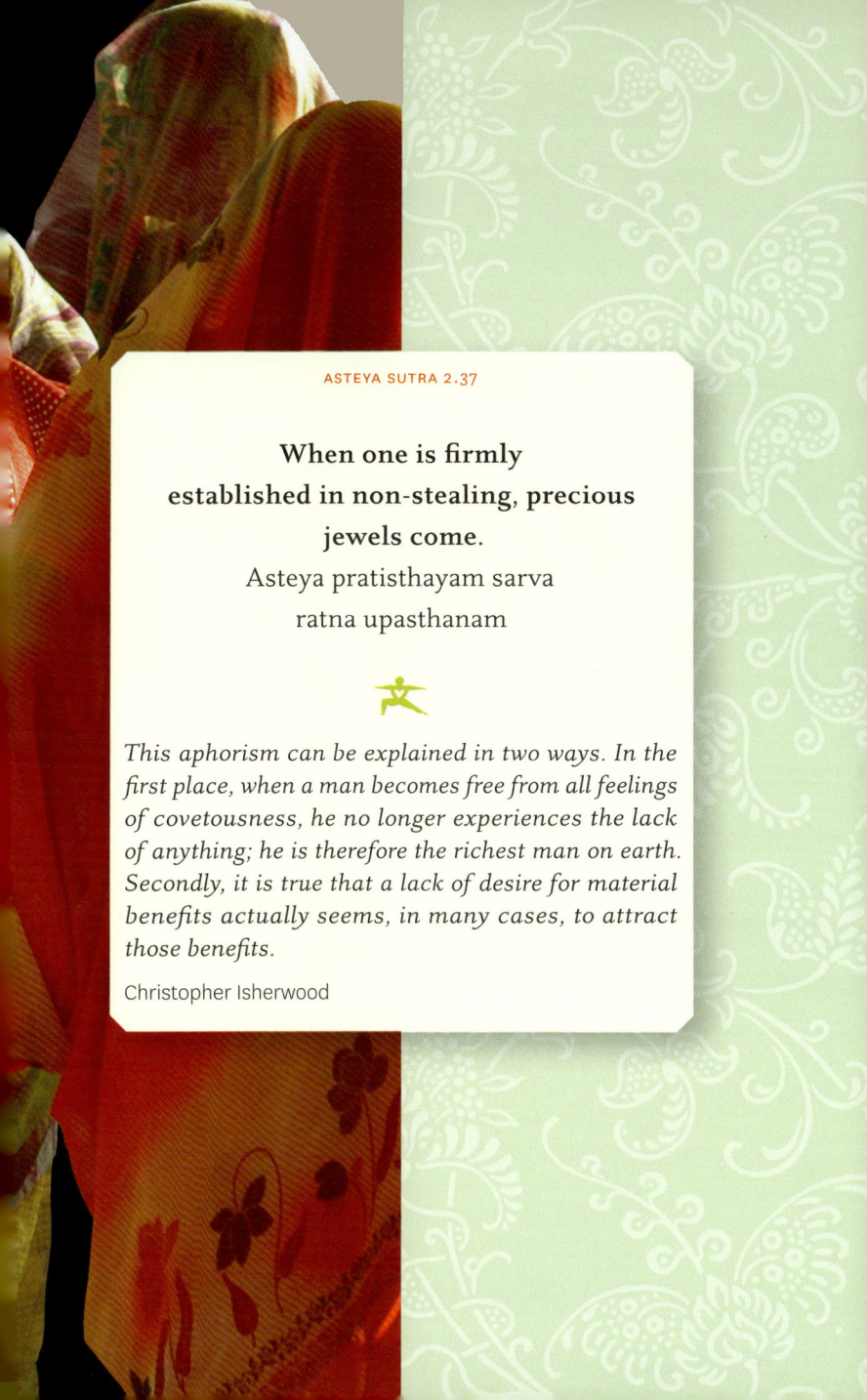

**When one is firmly
established in non-stealing, precious
jewels come.**

Asteya pratisthayam sarva
ratna upasthanam

*This aphorism can be explained in two ways. In the
first place, when a man becomes free from all feelings
of covetousness, he no longer experiences the lack
of anything; he is therefore the richest man on earth.
Secondly, it is true that a lack of desire for material
benefits actually seems, in many cases, to attract
those benefits.*

Christopher Isherwood

When one is firmly
established in moderation, vitality
is gained.
Brahmacarya pratisthayam
virya labhah

Brahmacharya is frequently translated as celibacy or abstinence, but actually its meaning is more comprehensive than refraining from sexual activity. Rather, it actually means one who is brahmacharya; this means one whose actions are all dedicated to God, one whose actions are all pure and holy. It means one whose attention, energy and life are focused on God . . . It means restraint. It means moderation. It means that the purpose of life is much greater and far deeper than continually fulfilling one's sexual urges. It means that all of our relationships should be ones in which we are moving closer and closer to the Divine.

H. H. Pujya Swami Chidanand Saraswatiji

**When one is established
in non-possessiveness, we gain knowledge
of our past and future lives.**
Aparigraha sthairye janma kathamta
sambodhah

*Aparigraha literally means "non-hoarding." It means
don't take more than you need in any area of life.
Mahatma Gandhiji said it beautifully: "There is more
than enough for everyone's need, but not enough for
any man's greed." It means, live simply. Use only that
which you require. Purchase only that which is essential.
The more we try to accumulate, the more we acquire,
the more we get bogged down, and the more difficulties
we face. So, travel light in life, and you will find that
you progress quickly and easily.*

H. H. Pujya Swami Chidanand Saraswatiji

SAUCHA SUTRA 2.40

When purification is attained, there follows detachment from contact with one's own body and the bodies of others.

Saucat sva anga jugupsa parair asamsargah

Saucha means "cleanliness and purity," but it does not simply imply that one must bathe each day and keep one's fingernails clean. Rather, it pertains to a deeper level of purity—purity on the inside, purity of thought and action. We must purify our thoughts through japa, meditation, and the practice of positive thinking. We must purify our lives by ensuring that our actions are models of integrity, dharma, and righteousness . . . True saucha means refraining from putting anything impure into our being—this includes everything ranging from drugs and cigarettes to negative gossip to violent rock-music lyrics to pornography.

H. H. Pujya Swami Chidanand Saraswatiji

**From purity of consciousness, there
arises cheerfulness,
power of concentration, control of
the sense, and fitness for
Self-realization.**
Sattva suddhi saumanasya eka agrya
indriya jaya atma darsana
yogyatvani ca

*The first sign that you are becoming religious is that
you are becoming cheerful. When a man is gloomy, that
may be dyspepsia, but it is not religion. A pleasurable
feeling is the nature of the Sattva (i.e., the quality of
lightness). Everything is pleasurable to the Sattvika man,
and when this comes, know that you are progressing
in Yoga. To the Yogi everything is bliss; every human
face that he sees brings cheerfulness to him. That is
the sign of a virtuous man.*

Sri Swami Vivekananda

Contentment brings supreme happiness.

Santosat anuttamah sukha labhah

It is well worth analyzing the circumstances of those occasions on which we have been truly happy. For, as John Masefield says, "The days that make us happy make us wise." When we review them, we shall almost certainly find that they had one characteristic in common. There were times when, for this or that reason, we had temporarily ceased to feel anxious, when we lived—as we so seldom do—in the depths of the present moment without regretting the past or worrying about the future. This is what Patanjali means by contentment.

Christopher Isherwood

Austerities destroy impurities, and with the resulting perfection of the mind, body, and sense organs, physical and mental powers awaken.

Kaya indriya siddhir asuddhi
ksayat tapasah

To be satisfied with the minimum of necessities for a healthy living is Tapas, or austerity. One should not ask for more. Austerity is that discipline by which one feels internally contented with the barest of facilities in life. Tapas is what produces heat. It stirs energy or power within the Yogin. The practice of Brahmacharya and of the Yamas in general stimulates supernatural power. The Yamas themselves constitute an intense Tapas. In a broad sense, moderateness in life may be said to constitute Tapas.

Sri Swami Krishnananda

Through study of scriptures comes union with one's chosen diety.

Svadhyayad ista devata samprayogah

Again, svadhyaya, or spiritual study, means study of scriptures and any practice that is our own personal sadhana (i.e., practice) into which we've been initiated. Regular practice becomes study. By it we get ishta devata samprayogah—the vision, or darsan, of the Lord.

Sri Swami Satchidananda

Samadhi is obtained
through surrender to Isvara (God).

Samadhi siddhir isvara pranidhanat

Surrender to God implies acceptance of the divine ordinance and an abolition of one's own initiative to the extent that the seeker does not think individually but resigns himself to those circumstances which take place around him, without interfering with their occurrence. He does not wish to alter conditions but tolerates everything. He allows things to happen and does not wish to modify existence. To him, God is all. This is the essence of self-surrender in Yoga.

Sri Swami Krishnananda

Asana

The body is my temple and asanas are my prayers.

B. K. S. Iyengar

In ancient texts, such as the Upanishads, asana refers to "seat." The purpose of asana is to train the body so that it does not disturb the concentration of the yogi when sitting in meditation. In Sutra 2.46, Patanjali supports this view saying: "The posture should be steady and comfortable." Our asana practice should be used to train our bodies so that we can sit in meditation for a long period of time without becoming distracted by bodily tension, discomfort, and instability.

There are other benefits to practicing asana, such as making our bodies strong and healthy, supporting the practice of pranayama, and preparing our bodies for the demands of our Yoga practice.

When perfection in asana is achieved, Sutra 2.48 states that there is freedom from the dualities such as heat and cold, motion and stillness, and joy and sadness. B. K. S. Iyengar translates this sutra to mean that the dualities between body and mind, and between mind and soul are ended. Asana can lead us to the state of samadhi, which is non-dual awareness.

Modern science and Yoga both recognize the continuum of the body and the mind and their interaction with each other. When our bodies are calm and stable, our minds tend to be calm and stable. When our bodies are tense and constricted, our minds tend to be tense and constricted. If our minds are not calm and still, we cannot success-fully practice the inner path of Yoga- (i.e., concentration (dharana), meditation (dhyana), and absorption (samadhi)). Nor can we attain the goal of Yoga, which is to still the mind, as we know from Sutra 1.2.

Sutra 2.47 states that steadiness in asana may be accomplished through meditation on Ananta. What does this enigmatic sutra mean? According to Hindu mythology, Ananta is the great serpent who symbolizes the force that maintains the balance of Earth and keeps it in orbit around our sun. This force is similar to the one that works in a gyroscope—it stabilizes a moving body. Thus, meditation on balance (Ananta) brings stability to the posture.

Patanjali only devotes three sutras to asana, but he dedicates twenty sutras to the yamas and niyamas. Because of the emphasis on asana in Western Yoga practice, we might expect that it would play a more important role in the Yoga Sutras. However, in classical Yoga the pur-pose of asana is to support the practice of meditation rather than an end goal in itself.

We should understand the distinction between Hatha Yoga and classical Yoga. Hatha Yoga is based on the principle that changes in consciousness are brought about by changing the flow of energy channels inside the body. It emphasizes the purification of the body through asana because impurities obstruct the flow of these ener-gies. Some of the classic works on Hatha Yoga mention eighty-four important asanas. They give specific instuction on bodily purification techniques, as well as pranayama.

The Yoga Sutras do not contain any specific asanas but rather emphasize the qualities of right asana practice. The goal of asana in classical Yoga is to build a steady, comfortable posture so that bodily distractions will not disrupt our practice of pranayama and meditation.

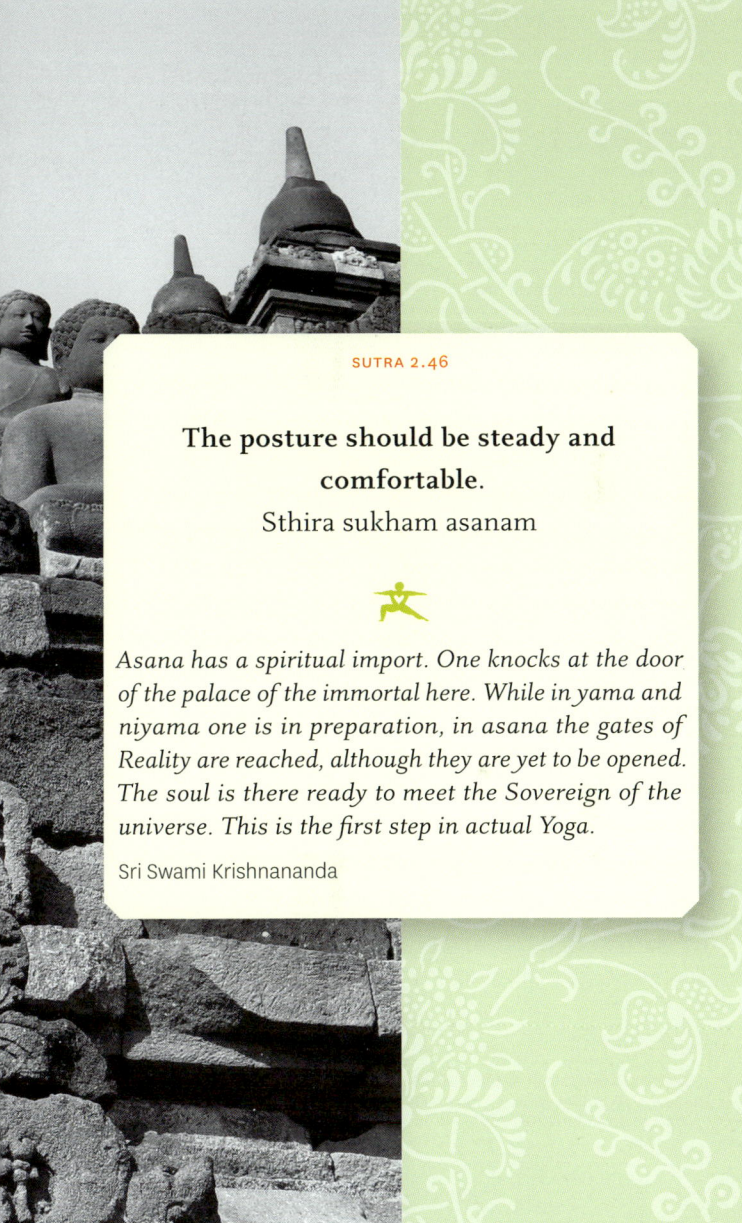

The posture should be steady and comfortable.

Sthira sukham asanam

Asana has a spiritual import. One knocks at the door of the palace of the immortal here. While in yama and niyama one is in preparation, in asana the gates of Reality are reached, although they are yet to be opened. The soul is there ready to meet the Sovereign of the universe. This is the first step in actual Yoga.

Sri Swami Krishnananda

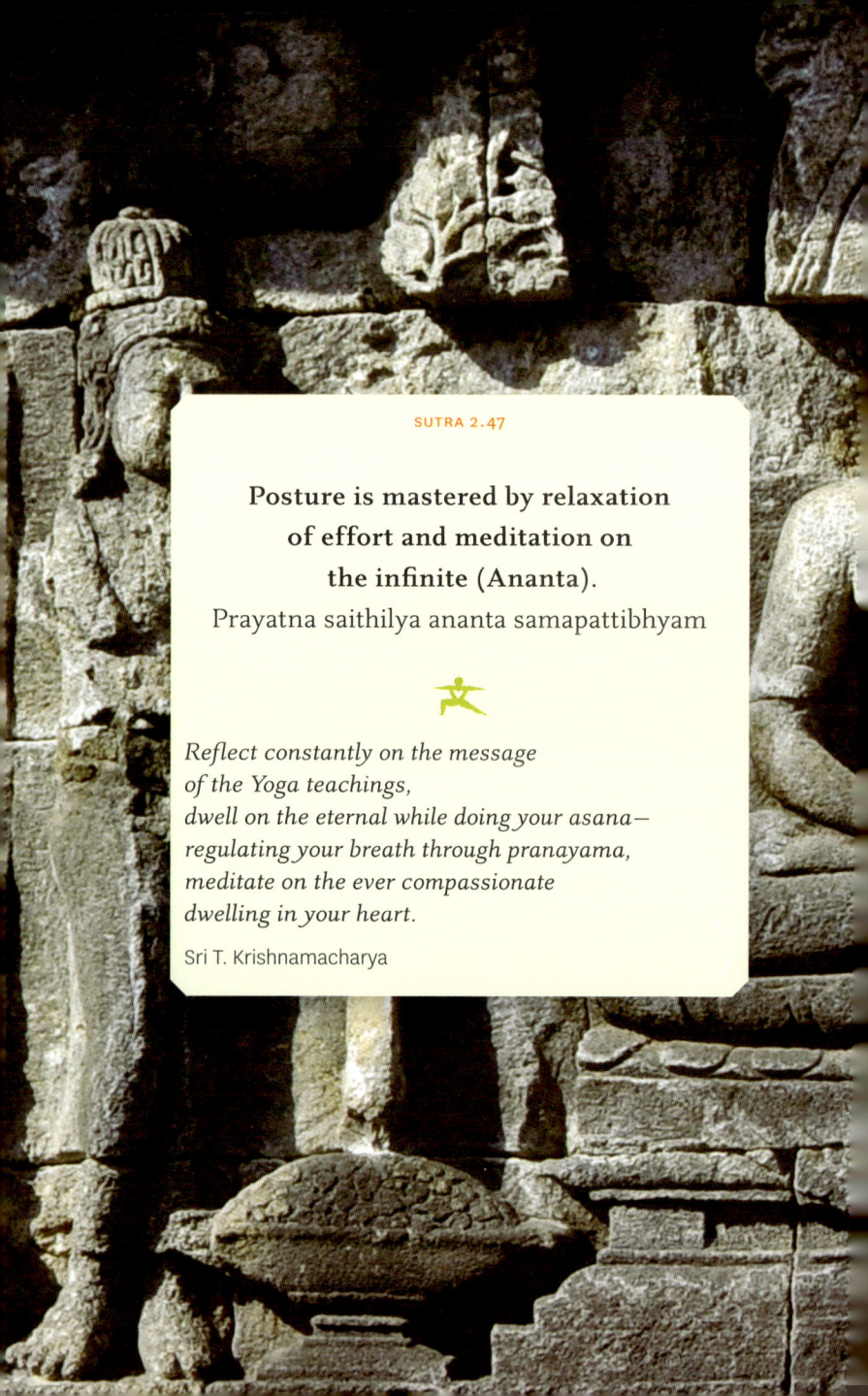

SUTRA 2.47

**Posture is mastered by relaxation
of effort and meditation on
the infinite (Ananta).**

Prayatna saithilya ananta samapattibhyam

*Reflect constantly on the message
of the Yoga teachings,
dwell on the eternal while doing your asana—
regulating your breath through pranayama,
meditate on the ever compassionate
dwelling in your heart.*

Sri T. Krishnamacharya

When posture is mastered, one is not disturbed by the dualities.

Tato dvandva anabhighatah

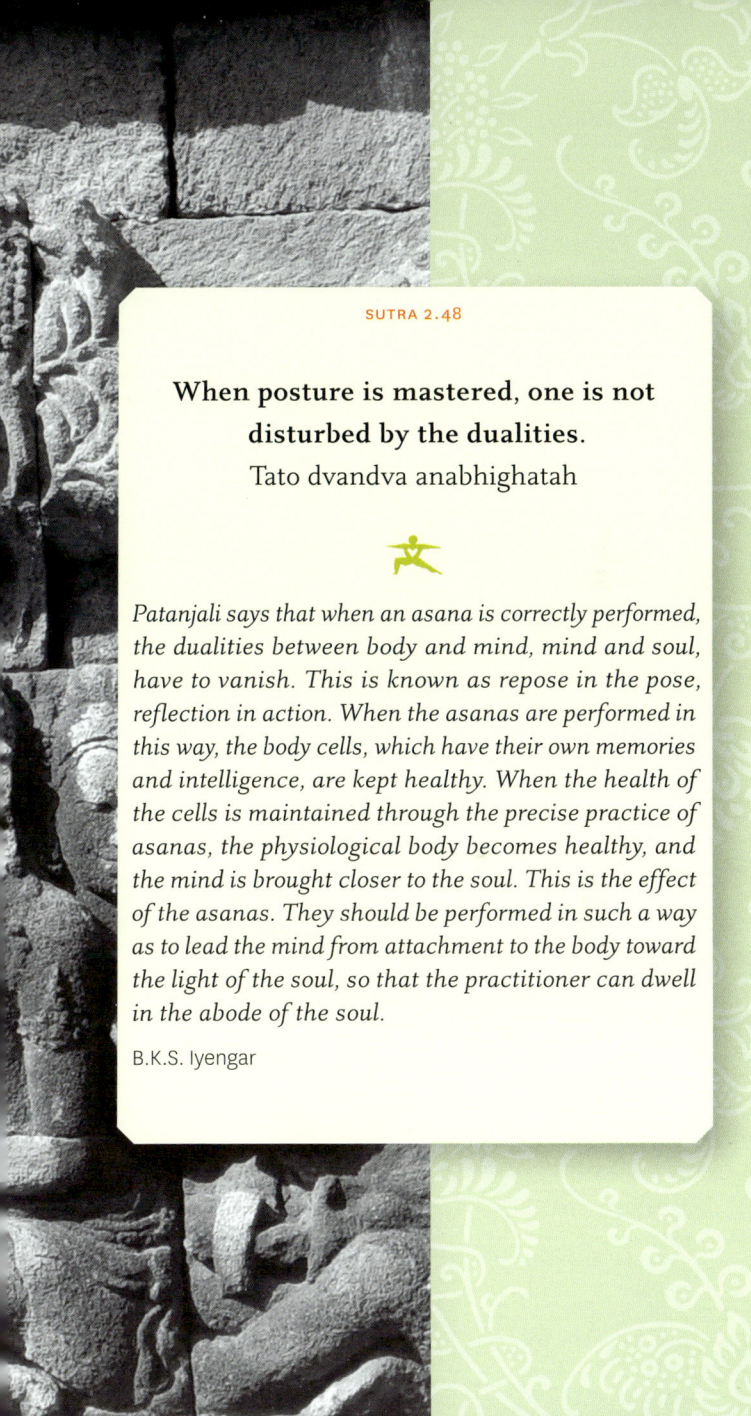

Patanjali says that when an asana is correctly performed, the dualities between body and mind, mind and soul, have to vanish. This is known as repose in the pose, reflection in action. When the asanas are performed in this way, the body cells, which have their own memories and intelligence, are kept healthy. When the health of the cells is maintained through the precise practice of asanas, the physiological body becomes healthy, and the mind is brought closer to the soul. This is the effect of the asanas. They should be performed in such a way as to lead the mind from attachment to the body toward the light of the soul, so that the practitioner can dwell in the abode of the soul.

B.K.S. Iyengar

Pranayama and Dharana

As we learn to get in touch with our breath—our prana, our life force—we come into contact with the very divine force which sustains our existence and unites us with the rest of the world. Prana literally means the life force, the energy, which flows through all. It can be physical energy, mental energy, intellectual energy, or even magnetic or heat energy! Ayama means expansion. So pranayama is the extension, the stretching, the prolonging of our life force and energy.

Pranayama teaches us to be calm, collected, and centered. As the breath becomes still, slow, deep, and steady, we find that in our lives also we become steady and still. We learn not to be ruffled by the ups and downs of life. We feel deeply connected to the very force that flows through each of us, giving us life.

H. H. Pujya Swami Chidanand Saraswatiji

Prana is the universal energy or life force. It is the sum total of all energy that is manifested in the universe. Prana is the connecting link between matter and energy, and it enters the body through the breath. Pranayama is the practice of working with prana by restraining or regulating the breath. By manipulating the breath, we can regulate the flow of prana in our bodies and minds.

In Yoga, breath control equals mental control. Sri Swami Satchidananda said: "By regulating prana, we regulate our minds, because the two always go together. If one is controlled, the other is automatically controlled as well. That is why pranayama is given by Patanjali and is so very important." The important role that pranayama plays in Yoga practice is based upon this close relationship between prana and mind.

You may have practiced pranayama in Yoga class when your teacher encouraged you to use *ujjayi* breathing (ocean sounding breathing) during your asana practice or *nadi shodhana* (alternate nostril breathing) as you prepared for meditation.

Asana practice prepares our bodies for pranayama. As it progresses, our bodies naturally begin to prepare for pranayama because the breath moves more slowly, rhythmically, and intentionally. Because prana pervades the entire physical body, asana and pranayama should be practiced together.

Pranayama supports our practice of concentration (dharana). In Sutra 3.1, Patanjali defines dharana as the continuous, uninterrupted flow of concentration directed toward an object. When we are practicing mindfulness, we are practicing dharana. The teaching by Thich Nhat Hanh quoted in Sutra 2.53 is a beautiful illustration of the practice of dharana when eating an orange.

**After perfection of posture
is achieved, the movements of
inhalation and exhalation should be
controlled. This is pranayama.**
Tasmin sati svasa
prasvasayor gati vicchedah
pranayamah

*Posture becoming established, a Yogi, master of himself,
eating salutary and moderate food, should practise
Pranayama, as instructed by his guru. Respiration being
disturbed, the mind becomes disturbed. By restraining
respiration, the Yogi gets steadiness of mind.*

Hatha Yoga Pradipika

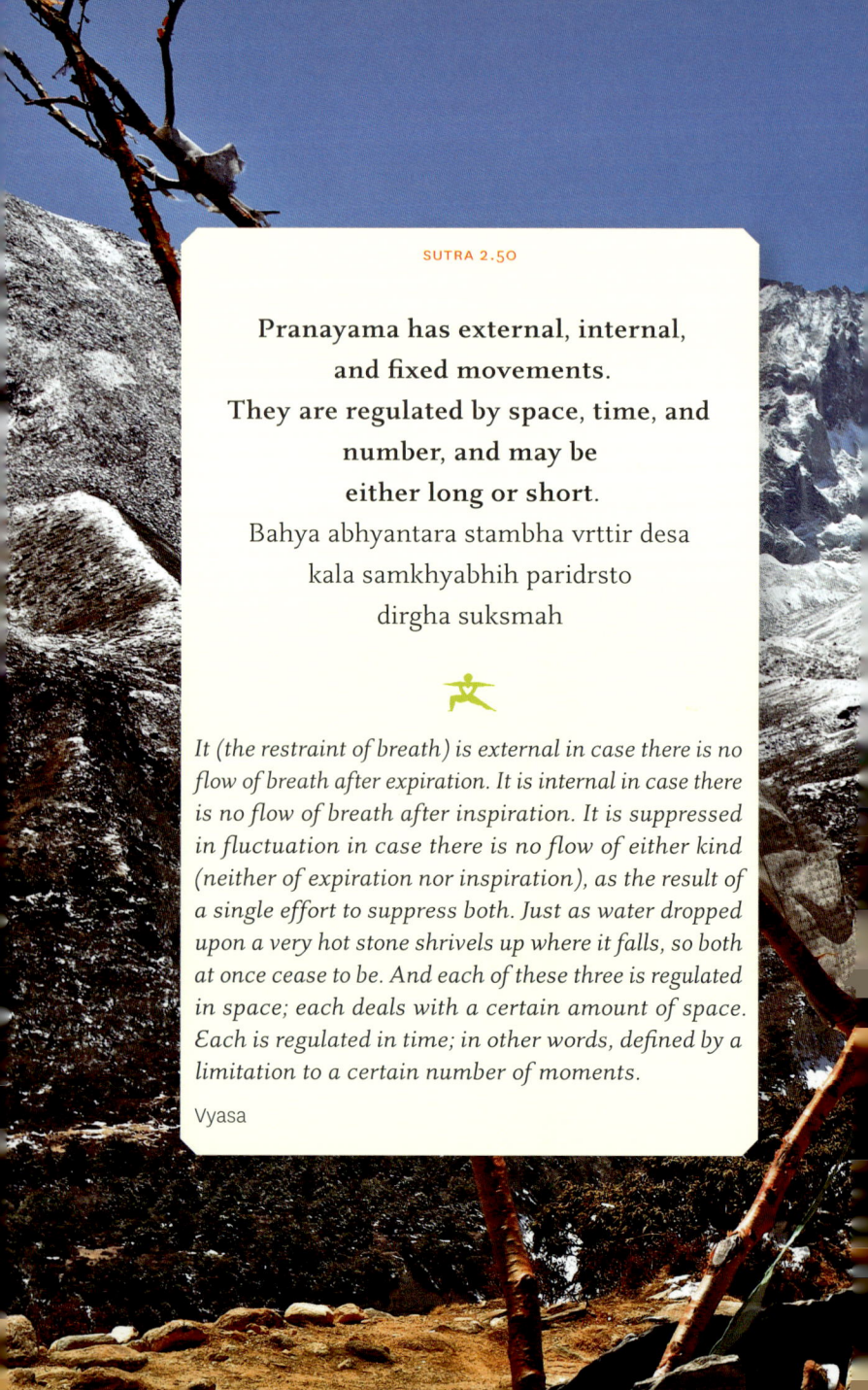

Pranayama has external, internal, and fixed movements. They are regulated by space, time, and number, and may be either long or short.
Bahya abhyantara stambha vrttir desa kala samkhyabhih paridrsto dirgha suksmah

It (the restraint of breath) is external in case there is no flow of breath after expiration. It is internal in case there is no flow of breath after inspiration. It is suppressed in fluctuation in case there is no flow of either kind (neither of expiration nor inspiration), as the result of a single effort to suppress both. Just as water dropped upon a very hot stone shrivels up where it falls, so both at once cease to be. And each of these three is regulated in space; each deals with a certain amount of space. Each is regulated in time; in other words, defined by a limitation to a certain number of moments.

Vyasa

There is a fourth kind of pranayama that transcends the others and operates in the external and internal realms.

Bahya abhyantara visaya aksepi
caturthah

Practice pranayama with attention.
Then, when the breath becomes long and smooth,
the mind is ready for meditation.

Sri. T. Krishnamacharya

As a result of this, the veil covering the inner light dwindles away.

Tatah ksiyate prakasa avaranam

In the case of the yogin who is practicing restraint of breath, the karma capable of covering discriminative thinking dwindles away. Therefore, by practicing restraint of breath, his karma which covers the light, together with its bondage to the round-of-rebirth, becomes powerless. And from moment to moment it dwindles away.

Vyasa

And the mind becomes fit for concentration.

Dharanasu ca yogyata manasah

Take the time to eat an orange in mindfulness. If you eat an orange in forgetfulness, caught in your anxiety and sorrow, the orange is not really there. But if you bring your mind and body together to produce true presence, you can see that the orange is a miracle. See the orange blossoms in the orange, and the rain and the sun that have gone through the orange blossoms. Put a section in your mouth, close your mouth mindfully, and with mindfulness feel the juice coming out of the orange. Do you have the time to do so? If you think you don't have time to eat an orange like this, what are you using that time for? Are you using your time to worry or using your time to live?

Thich Nhat Hanh

Pratyahara: Withdrawal of the Senses

Even as a tortoise draws in its limbs, the wise can draw in their senses at will. Aspirants abstain from sense pleasures, but they still crave for them. These cravings all disappear when they see the highest goal. Even of those who tread the path, the stormy senses can sweep off the mind. They live in wisdom who subdue their senses and keep their minds ever absorbed in me.

Bhagavad Gita, Chapter Two, Verses 58–60

Pratyahara is the withdrawal of our senses from contact with the external world and the focusing of our attention inward. As long as we are immersed in the world, we are trapped in its web of endlessly changing sensations, attractions, and aversions. Our experience of sight, sound, taste, smell, and touch is so powerful that we identify with our minds and our bodies. We think these sensations are who we really are. We lose sight of our true Self. This is spiritual ignorance.

In Chapter 2, Verse 60 of the Bhagavad Gita it is written, "Even of those who tread the path, the stormy senses can sweep off the mind. They live in wisdom who subdue their senses and keep their minds ever absorbed in me."

Our true Self speaks to us in subtle and quiet ways. We cannot access our true Self unless we quiet our senses. Since Yoga is the practice of stilling the noise in our minds, pratyahara is an essential practice. Unfortunately, pratyahara tends to be neglected in Western Yoga practice because most studios place a heavy emphasis on asana, and many students feel that Yoga is asana.

We are subjected to a relentless barrage of visual and auditory noise from mass media, social media, suburban sprawl, construction, and traffic. The result is that our senses become overloaded, and we become closed, constricted, and numb. We work faster and harder and multitask to keep up. We become obsessed with "doing" rather than "being." The inevitable result is stress and absorption in our daily routines and our to-do lists. This is the very opposite of the state we are trying to attain through the practice of Yoga. We need stillness, quiet, and peace to enter the state of Yoga.

Sri Satchidananda said: "The senses are like a mirror. Turned outward, they reflect outside; turned inward, they reflect the pure light. By themselves the senses are innocent, but when allowed to turn outside, they attract everything and transfer those messages to the mind, making it restless. Turned inward, they find peace by taking the form of the mind itself."

Pratyahara is the practice of switching off our senses and focusing our minds within. It is the practice of withdrawing from the world into a place of quiet so we can access our Yogic minds. Pratyahara can involve many different practices.

One practice is to experience nature. Spend time in the mountains, the seashore, or at a lake. Take a hike or a walk. Find a place of quiet

and allow your senses to rest and your mind to move within. Move slowly, observe carefully the sights and sounds, breathe deeply, and practice mindfulness. Another practice is to take a spiritual retreat.

Pratyahara is the final limb of the five external practices of Yoga (i.e., yama, niyama, pranayama, asana, and pratyahara). The focus of all these practices is to allow our attention to withdraw from the outside world and to move within. They remove the sources of things that disturb our minds so we can reside in our true Self.

The moral and societal disturbances are eliminated through the practice of the yamas and the niyamas. The disturbances flowing from the physical body are eliminated through the practice of asana. The disturbances caused by prana are removed through the practice of pranayama. Finally, the practice of pratyahara reduces the disturbances caused by our senses as we engage with the outside world.

After we have mastered the external practices, we will be ready for the last three limbs of Yoga. These are known as the internal practices and are dharana, dhyana, and samadhi. They are described at the beginning of Pada Three.

Pratyahara is when the senses withdraw themselves from their respective sense objects and imitate, as it were, the nature of the mind.

Sva visaya asamprayoge cittasya sva rupa anukara iva indriyanam pratyaharah

Just as when the king-bee flies up, the bees fly after him, and when he settles down, they settle down after him. So when the mind-stuff is restricted, the organs are restricted. This then is the withdrawal of the senses.

Vyasa

As a result of this withdrawal, there is supreme mastery over the senses.

Tatah parama vasyata indriyanam

Know the Self to be sitting in the chariot, the body to be the chariot, the intellect (buddhi) the charioteer, and the mind the reins. The senses they call the horses, the objects of the senses their roads.

He who has no understanding and whose mind (the reins) is never firmly held, his senses (horses) are unmanageable, like vicious horses of a charioteer. But he who has understanding and whose mind is always firmly held, his senses are under control, like good horses of a charioteer.

But he who has understanding for his charioteer and who holds the reins of the mind, he reaches the end of his journey, and that is the highest place of Vishnu.

Katha Upanishad, Chapter 1, Verses 3-12

पधारे सभी पूज्य संतों, आदरणीय अतिथियों का हा

Vibhuti Pada

The vibhuti are all the accomplishments which come as by-products of your Yoga practice.

Sri Swami Satchidananda

The Vibhuti Pada is concerned with the three internal practices and the extraordinary powers that may come to a very advanced yogi after long and dedicated practice.

The three internal practices are: *dharana*, *dhyana*, and *samadhi*. These are the last three limbs of Patanjali's Astanga Yoga and are collectively known as *samyama*. Dharana means focusing attention. Dhyana is the steady continuous flow of attention toward an object. The ultimate goal of yoga, samadhi, is defined as when the object of meditation merges with the person doing the meditation.

The analogy of contemplating a diamond is often used to explain samyama. When one meditates upon a diamond, one first sees with great clarity the diamond itself. This is dharana. As meditation continues, one becomes aware of light glowing from the center of the diamond, and as this light grows, the awareness of the diamond as an object diminishes. This is dhyana. When only the light remains without a source, the final state of samadhi is attained.

The remainder of Pada Three is concerned with an explanation of the siddhis, or powers, that yogis may achieve as they expand their consciousness.

These powers include knowledge of the speech of all creatures, knowledge of previous births, mind reading, the ability to become invisible, knowledge of one's own death, great strength, knowledge of remote or hidden things and realms of the universe, knowledge of the solar system and the stars, expansion of the power of the senses, the ability to enter the body of another, the power to levitate, divine hearing and radiance, the power to travel through the sky, and mastery of the elements.

Patanjali warns that these powers are obstacles to attaining the highest goals of Yoga.

Samyama-Dharana, Dhyana and Samadhi

It should be clear from what has been said previously in dealing with Dharana, Dhyana, and Samadhi that these are really different phases of the same mental process, each succeeding stage differing from the preceding in the depth of concentration which has been attained and the more complete isolation of the object of contemplation from distractions. The complete process beginning with Dharana and ending in Samadhi is called Samyama in Yogic terminology, and the practical mastery of its technique opens the door not only to knowledge of all kinds but also to powers and superphysical accomplishments known as Siddhis.

I. K. Taimni

To summarize our journey through the Sutras, Pada One, the Samadhi Pada, was written to guide highly evolved beings in their practice. Pada One defines Yoga and the goal of practicing Yoga. It describes various states of samadhi as well as many meditational practices to reach those states. Pada Two, the Sadhana Pada, was written at a more basic level and was intended to guide beginning practitioners. It describes the external practices. These practices are yama, niyama, asana, pranayama, and pratyahara. It offers the practice of Kriya Yoga which is tapas (self-discipline), svadhyaya (study of spiritual texts), and Isvara pranidhanani (devotion). It also gives us Astanga Yoga, the eight-limbed path.

Pada Three, the Vibhuti Pada, is concerned with the practices of internal yoga: dharana, dhyana, and samadhi. These three practices are collectively known as samyama. The first five limbs in Patanjali's Astanga Yoga are described in Pada Two, and the remaining three limbs are in Pada Three. Pada Three also describes the many yogic siddhis or powers that some advanced practitioners may attain.

Concentration (dharana) is fixing the mind on a single place.

Desa bandhas cittasya dharana

Dharana—the next step—single-minded concentration. Single-pointness. Asana taught us to control the body. Pranayama taught us to control the breath. Pratyahara taught us to control the senses. Now dharana teaches us to control the mind. In dharana, there are a wide variety of objects of concentration one can use. A burning candle, an image of the divine, the ocean, the tip of one's own nose, the center between one's eyebrows, the sound of a mantra, these are all common objects. The point is to focus, to stop the incessant wanderings of the mind. To channel all thought-power in one direction. To teach us to be the masters of our own minds.

H. H. Pujya Swami Chidanand Saraswatiji

Meditation (dhyana) is the continuous flow of consciousness toward an object.

Tatra pratyaya ekatanata dhyanam

People frequently confuse concentration with meditation. They confuse dharana with dhyana. In concentration, there is a subject and an object. You, the subject, are concentrating on a candle, or an image of God, or the tip of your nose. These are objects of concentration. In meditation, the object disappears. The subject disappears. All becomes one. Rather than focusing on a mantra, you and the mantra become one. In meditation, all borders, boundaries, and separation between ourselves and the universe begin to disappear. We begin to realize the inherent oneness of all beings and all of creation.

H. H. Pujya Swami Chidanand Saraswatiji

Samadhi is deep absorption in the
object without thought of the
self (who is meditating).
Then, only the essential nature of the
object shines forth in the mind.
Tad eva artha matra nirbhasam sva
rupa sunya iva samadih

*It is only in the super sensuous perception of samadhi
that we see an object in the truth of its own nature,
absolutely free from the distortions of our imagination. Samadhi is, in fact, much more than perception;
it is direct knowledge. When Sri Ramakrishna told
Vivekananda, "I see God more real than I see you," he
was speaking the literal truth. For Ramakrishna meant
that he saw God in samadhi, while he saw Vivekananda
with the eyes of his ordinary sense-perception, which
must necessarily retain a measure of distortion.*

Christopher Isherwood

**The practice of these three together
(dharana, dhyana, and samadhi)
on one object is called
samyama.**
Trayam ekatra samyamah

*It is necessary to keep in mind two facts about Samyama.
First, it is a continuous process and the passage from
one stage to another is not marked by any abrupt change
in consciousness. Secondly, the time taken in reaching
the last stage depends entirely upon the progress made
by the Yogi. The beginner may have to spend hours and
days in reaching the final stage, while the adept can
pass into it almost instantaneously and effortlessly. As
Samadhi does not involve any movement in space but
merely sinking, as it were, towards the centre of one's
own consciousness, time is not an essential factor in
the process.*

I. K. Taimni

Through mastery of samyama, the light of knowledge dawns.

Taj jayat prajna alokah

The knowledge gained by samyamah is direct and intuitive. It is a bursting forth of the light—the reality or essential nature—of the object of meditation.

Reverend Jaganath Carrera

Footnotes and Credits

INTRODUCTION

Note: Some of the quotes within the body of the book were shortened because of graphic design considerations. We have included the expanded text of these quotes within this Appendix.

Georg Feuerstein, *The Yoga Sutra of Patanjali, A New Translation and Commentary* (Rochester, Vermont: Inner Traditions, 1979), viii.

H. H. Swami Chidanand Saraswatiji, *Holy Days* (2004), 140.

I. K. Taimni, *The Science Of Yoga* (Wheaton, Il: Quest Books 1999), 3.

Vyaas Houston, *Sanskrit and the Yoga Sutras* (http://www. americansanskrit.com/read/a_sutras.php).

Sri Swami Satchidananda, *The Yoga Sutras of Patanjali* (Integral Yoga Publications, 1978), 47.

Below are some resources for chants of the Yoga Sutras:

Kausthub Desikachar, Patanjali's Yoga Sutras (Swathi Soft Solutions, 2008) (available in iTunes Store)

Patanjali's Yoga Sutras: The Original Master's Eight Steps of Yoga (Times Music, India 2005) (available in iTunes Store)

PADA ONE: SAMADHI PADA

B. K. S. Iyengar, *Light on the Yoga Sutras of Patanjali* (San Francisco, California: Thorsons, 1996), 4.

H. H. Pujya Swami Chidanand Saraswatiji, *Yoga, The Essence of Life*, 15.

SUTRAS 1.1–1.4 INTRODUCTION

Eknath Easwaran, *The Upanishads—The Chandogya Upanishad*, Chapter VI, Verses 2.2-2.3 (Tomales, California: Nilgiri Press 1987), 183.

Jonathan Star, *Rumi—In the Arms of the Beloved* (New York: Tarcher/Penguin 2008), 181.

Ken Wilber, *The Simple Feeling of Being* (Boston, Massachusetts: Shambhala 2004), 15.

Ramana Maharshi, *The Essential Teachings of Ramana Maharshi* (Vista, California: Inner Directions, 2002), 26.

Jaganath Carrera, *Inside the Yoga Sutras* (Integral Yoga Publications 2005), 14.

Jaganath Carrera, *Inside the Yoga Sutras*, 19.

SUTRA 1.1

Temple devoted to Hanuman and Rama, Rishikesh, India (courtesy of the author)

Sri Swami Satchidananda, *The Yoga Sutras of Patanjali*, 3.

SUTRA 1.2

A Saiva yogi seated on a tiger's skin in front of a Siva temple (19th Century); courtesy of the British Library Board (Image illuminating Sutra 1.2)

Swami Rajarshi Muni, Yoga: The Ultimate Spiritual Path (Woodbury, Minnesota: Llewellyn Publications 2002), 130. (Quotation relating to Sutra 1.2)

Dudh Pokhari, Gokyo's Third Lake, Nepal; permission by Shutterstock (Image illuminating citta vrtti)

Swami Vivekananda, *Patanjali Yoga Sutras* (Sanskrit text with transliteration, translation and commentary), 11. (Quotation relating to citta vrtti)

Rock garden at the Ryoan-ji temple in Kyoto, Japan; permission by Shutterstock (Image illuminating nirodha)

Eknath Easwaran, *The Upanishads* (Tomales California: Nilgiri Press, 2007), 38. (Quotation relating to nirodha)

SUTRA 1.3

Buddha Statue—Ayutthaya, Thailand; permission of Shutterstock. Background to Buddha image: The Orion Nebula, M42; courtesy of NASA, ESA and STScI.

I. K. Taimni, *The Science Of Yoga*, 16.

SUTRA 1.4

Temple in Tamil Nadu, India; courtesy of the author

Ramana Maharshi, *The Essential Teachings of Ramana Maharshi*, 106.

SUTRAS 1.5–1.11 INTRODUCTION

Eknath Easwaran, *The Bhagavad Gita* (Tomales, California: Nilgiri Press 2007), 143.

Simulation of an ion collision; courtesy of the European Organization for Nuclear Research

SUTRA 1.5

Statues of the Saints, Santa Fe, New Mexico; courtesy of the author

Sri Swami Satchidananda, *The Yoga Sutras of Patanjali*, 9–10.

SUTRA 1.6

Temple Mural, Lumbini, Nepal; courtesy of the author

Sri Muni describes the activities of the vrttis as follows:

"As an individual involves him or herself in the daily activities of life, his or her citta (consciousness) acts in concert with his or her mind, ego, and intellect to experience and record all of the impressions received through the five jnanendriyas (cognitive senses). Because an individual identifies with these experiences, considering them to be real, they create corresponding modifications, or vrttis, in his or her stream of consciousness. These 'chitta-vrttis' as they are called are theoretically of infinite variety because of the innumerable ways sensory input can be perceived, biased, interpolated, etc., to create inner experience. Sage Patanjali, however, has classified all vrttis into five broad categories of (i) pramana (right knowledge), (ii) viparyaya (wrong knowledge), (iii) vikalpa (imagination), (iv) nidra (sleep). and (v) smriti (memory)."

Swami Rajarshi Muni, Yoga: *The Ultimate Spiritual Path*, 130.

SUTRA 1.7

12th Century Persian Miniature Image; courtesy of Walters Art Museum-Islamic Manuscript Digital Project

"Pramana or right knowledge is awareness of things as they are. Perception, inference and verbal testimony are the three primary ways of right knowledge. Some add comparison, presumption, and non-apprehension to the usual avenues of such knowledge. How do we know that there is an object in front of us? We acquire this knowledge through direct sensory contact. This is perception. And when we see muddy water in a river, we suppose that there must have been rains uphill. This knowledge we gather by inference.

The words of others in whom we have faith also convey to us true knowledge as, for example, when we believe that there is an elephant in the nearby city, on hearing of it from a reliable friend, though we might not have actually seen it with our eyes. All these methods together form what goes by the name of Pramana or direct proof of dependable knowledge."

Sri Swami Krishnananda, *The Yoga System* (The Divine Life Society, 1992), 2.

SUTRA 1.8

Image of coiled rope; permission by Shutterstock

H. H. Dalai Lama, *How to Practice: The Way to A Meaningful Life* (New York: Atria,2003), 139.

SUTRA 1.9

Seated man smoking water pipe, unknown origin; courtesy of Library of Congress Digital Archives 1898-1946

"False imaginations rise from the consideration of appearances: things are discriminated as to form, signs, and shape; as to having color, warmth, humidity, motility, or rigidity. False imagination consists in becoming attached to these appearances and their names. By attachment to objects is meant the getting attached to inner and outer things as if they were real. By attachment to names is meant the recognition in these inner and outer things of the characteristic marks of individuation and generality, and to regard them as definitely belonging to the names of the objects.

By reason of clinging to these false imaginations there is multitudinousness of appearances which are imagined to be real but which are only imaginary. To illustrate: when a magician depending on grass, wood, shrubs, and creepers exercises his art, many shapes and beings take form that are only magically created; sometimes they even make figures that have bodies and that move and act like human beings; they are variously and fancifully discriminated but there is no reality in them; everyone but children and the simple-minded know that they are not real."

Dwight Goddard, *A Buddhist Bible—The Favorite Scriptures of the Zen Sect* (Dwight Goddard 1932), D.T. Suzuki, Translation of The Lankavatara Sutra (http://www.sacred-texts.com/bud/ bb/bb08. htm), 65-66.

SUTRA 1.10

Photon Crawfish; courtesy of Ken Adams

Ramana Maharshi, *The Collected Works of Sri Ramana Maharshi*, No.8, 38 (oral transcriptions; no copyright information).

SUTRA 1.11

Katsushika, Hokusai, Koshu Kajikazawa (1760-1849); courtesy of Library of Congress Digital Archives

"The part of the brain in which memory resides is paved with all sorts of images, most of the past, covering it like a veil. When something new is dropped in that thick layer of thoughts and sensations, it is obviously more difficult to remember. Such an occupied container is not free to receive, as all sorts of distractions are interfering. Instead, when there is space one retains and remembers more easily. Memory is there. It contains our past conditioning: our childhood, our education, our culture (from which taste is molded), our experiences, our knowledge, our environment, our country, our family, our friends. Let us leave all this alone and not use those things, not exploit them or speculate upon them. They should remain there in a complete immobility, like the background of a picture or a map. Not to carry them along is a blessing!"

Vanda Scaravelli, *Awakening the Spine* (San Francisco, California: Harper One 1991), 77-83.

SUTRAS 1.12–1.16 INTRODUCTION

Eknath Easwaran, *The Bhagavad Gita,* 94.

B. K. S. Iyengar, *Light on the Yoga Sutras of Patanjali*, 62.

Japanese Drawing, Warrior, full-length, facing left, with bow drawn, about to shoot an arrow at a target, Kano (1878); courtesy of Library of Congress Digital Archives

SUTRA 1.12

Lotus Flower Garden, Lumbini, Nepal; courtesy of the author

Eknath Easwaran, *The Bhagavad Gita*, 128.

SUTRA 1.13

Konen, Uehara-Hato Zu (Waves); courtesy of Library of Congress Digital Archives, 1900–1920

"Let us take whatever comes as prasad, as a gift from God. Let us remain calm and steady in the face of both prosperity and misfortune. We must not lose our vital energy in this constant action and reaction to everyone around us. But how? How to remain unaffected by the waves of life? This is called spiritual practice! I always say that one of the best ways to learn 'no reaction' is through silence. When we are anxious, angry, tense or frustrated, we tend to say things which we later regret; we tend to let our words fuel the reaction in our hearts. So, let us learn the power of silence. Silence on the outside will lead to silence on the inside. This is why so many saints and other spiritual people have 'silence time;' it's a time of remembering that we are more than our reactions, a time of tuning in to the Divine Insurance Company, a time of charging our inner batteries. So, let us learn to meet life's waves with silence— that will make 'no reaction' much easier to achieve."

H. H. Pujya Swami Chidanand Saraswatiji, *Drops of Nectar* (Parmarth Niketan, 2004), 80.

SUTRA 1.14

Arunachala, India; courtesy of the author

T. K. V. Desikachar, *The Heart of Yoga* (Rochester, Vermont: Inner Traditions 1995), 222.

SUTRA 1.15

Skychurch Zero G; courtesy of Ken Adams

"Mahamati, the ignorant and simple-minded, not knowing that the world is only some-thing seen of the mind itself, cling to the multitudinousness of external objects, cling to the notions of being and nonbeing, oneness and otherness, bothness and not-bothness, existence and non-existence, eternity and non-eternity, and think that they have a self-nature of their own, all of which rises from the discriminations of the mind and is perpetuated by habit-energy, and from which they are given over to false imagination.

It is like the city of the Gandharvas, which the unwitting take to be a real city though it is not so in fact. The city appears as in a vision owing to their attachment to the memory of a city preserved in the mind as a seed; the city can thus be said to be both existent and non-existent.

It is like a man dreaming in his sleep of a country that seems to be filled with various men, women, elephants, horses, cars, pedestrians, villages, towns, hamlets, cows, buffalos, man-sions, woods, mountains, rivers and lakes, and who moves about in that city until he is awakened. As he lies half awake, he recalls the city of his dreams and reviews his experiences there; what do you think, Mahamati, is this dreamer who is letting his mind dwell upon the various unrealities he has seen in his dream-is he to be considered wise or foolish? It is like a mirror reflecting colors and images as determined by conditions but without any partiality. It is like the echo of the wind that gives the sound of a human voice. It is like a mirage of moving water seen in a desert."

Dwight Goddard, *A Buddhist Bible—The Favorite Scriptures of the Zen Sect* (Dwight Goddard 1932), D.T. Suzuki, Translation of The Lankavatara Sutra, 48–49 (http://www.sacred-texts.com/bud/ bb/ bb08.htm)

SUTRA 1.16

Handaka Sonja (a disciple of Buddha), sitting next to a flower and holding a bowl to collect rain; courtesy of Library of Congress Digital Archives, 1830-1868.

Zen Master Dogen, *The Treasury of Eyes of the True Teaching* (http://www.sacred-texts.com/bud/zen/poems.htm), 69–70.

SUTRAS 1.17–1.19 INTRODUCTION

Hatha Yoga Pradipika, Chapter IV, Verse 5 (Translation Pancham Sinh 1914) (http://www.sacred-texts.com/hin/hyp/index. htm#contents)

Swami Vivekananda, *Patanjali Yoga Sutras*, 21.

Sri Swami Satchidananda, *The Yoga Sutras of Patanjali*, 31–32.

Sri Swami Krishnananda, *The Study and Practice of Yoga*, (http://www.swami-krishnananda.org/patanjali/raja_50.html) Part I, Chapter 50.

SUTRA 1.17

Acoma Pueblo, New Mexico; courtesy of the author

Raghavan Iyer, "A Commentary on the Yoga Sutras" (http://www. atmajyoti.org/sw_commentary_on_yoga_sutras.asp).

SUTRA 1.18

Yosemite, California; courtesy of the author

Sri Swami Satchidananda, *The Yoga Sutras of Patanjali*, 35.

SUTRA 1.19

Acoma Pueblo, New Mexico; courtesy of the author

Swami Prabirthananda and Christopher Isherwood, *The Yoga Aphorisms of Patanjali, How to Know God, Translated With a New Commentary*, (Vedanta Society of Southern California 1953), 23.

SUTRAS 1.20–1.22 INTRODUCTION

F. Max Muller, *Ramakrishna—His Life and Sayings*, (http://www. sacred-texts.com/ hin/rls/index.htm) Number 136.

Baba Hari Dass, *Fire Without Fuel* (Santa Cruz, California: Sri Rama Publishing, 1986), 79.

SUTRA 1.20

Sadhu, India; permission by Shutterstock

Eknath Easwaran, *The Bhagavad Gita*, (Nilgiri Press 1985), 142.

SUTRA 1.21

Tibet, courtesy of the author

Eknath Easwaran, The Upanishads, 117.

SUTRA 1.22

Temple priest, Udaipur, India; courtesy of the author

Eknath Easwaran, *The Upanishads*, 177.

INTRODUCTION TO SUTRAS 1.23–1.28

Rumi, *In the Arms of the Beloved*, translation by Jonathan Star (New York: Penguin Putnam, 1997), 170.

Songs of Kabir, translation by Rabindranath Tagore (New York: The Macmillan Company, 1915), 75.

Sri Swami Satchidananda, *The Yoga Sutras of Patanjali*, 82–83.

T. K. V. Desikachar, *The Heart of Yoga*, 129.

Stupa and Prayer Flags, Boudhanath Stupa, Kathmandu, India; courtesy of the author

SUTRA 1.23

The Offering of the Six Devas to the Tia Tan Buddha, Hong Kong. permission by Shutterstock

Sri Swami Satchidananda, *The Yoga Sutras of Patanjali,* 39.

SUTRA 1.24

Bodhisattva Guanyin, 12th Century, China; courtesy of Rijksmuseum, Amsterdam

SUTRA 1.25

Tibet Temple, courtesy of the author

Eknath Easwaran, *The Bhagavad Gita,* 234.

SUTRA 1.26

Ceiling of the Great Gate to the Taj Mahal; Agra, India (Darwaza-I rauza); courtesy of the author.

Songs of Kabir, Translated by Rabindranath Tagore, (The Macmillan Company, 1915), Chapter 2.38.

SUTRA 1.27

Rishikesh; India; courtesy of the author

Swami Nirmalananda Giri, *Om Yoga, Its Theory and Practice* (Atma Jyoti Press, 2006), 18.

SUTRA 1.28

Ralph T. H. Griffith, translator of *The Gayatri Mantra*, The Rig Veda Book 3, Chapter 62, Verse 10 (1896), http://www.sacred-texts. com/hin/rigveda/index.htm.

SUTRA 1.29–1.33 INTRODUCTION

Baba Hari Dass, *Fire Without Fuel*, 137.

F. Max Muller, *The Dhammapada, A Collection of Verses Being One of the Canonical Books of the Buddhists* (Oxford: The Clarendon Press 1881,) 4 (http://www.sacred-texts.com/bud/sbe10/sbe1003.htm).

Sri Swami Satchidananda, *The Yoga Sutras of Patanjali*, 54–55.

Ganesha, Katmandu, Nepal; courtesy of the author

SUTRA 1.29

Lord Rama, Rishikesh, India (Wall Mural); courtesy of the author

"One of the basic mantras is, of course, the word spelled OM. That sound is used because it runs from the back of your throat to your lips and contains the whole range of the voice, and it represents the total energy of the universe. This word is called the pravana, the name for the Ultimate Reality. And so in this way, if you chant it, and vary it, and keep it up for quite a long time, you find that the words will become pure sound. You won't be thinking about it; you won't have any images about the sound going on in your mind. You will become completely absorbed in the sound and find yourself living in an eternal now in which there is no past and there is no future, and there is no difference between you as knower and what you are as the known, between yourself and the world of nature outside you. It all becomes one doing, one happening."

Alan Watts, *The Essence of Alan Watts* (Berkeley, California: Celestial Arts, 1974) 56.

Statue of Kala Bhairab (Shiva in a fearsome manifestation), near Jagnannath Temple, Katmandu, Nepal; courtesy of the author

"As a fletcher makes straight his arrow, a wise man makes straight his trembling and unsteady thought, which is difficult to guard, difficult to hold back. As a fish taken from his watery home and thrown on dry ground, our thought trembles all over in order to escape the dominion of Mâra (the tempter).

It is good to tame the mind, which is difficult to hold in and flighty, rushing wherever it listeth; a tamed mind brings happiness. Let the wise man guard his thoughts, for they are difficult to perceive, very artful, and they rush wherever they list: thoughts well guarded bring happiness.

Those who bridle their mind, which travels far, moves about alone, is without a body, and hides in the chamber (of the heart), will be free from the bonds of Mâra (the tempter). If a man's thoughts are unsteady, if he does not know the true law, if his peace of mind is troubled, his knowledge will never be perfect."

F. Max Muller, *The Dhammapada*, 12 (http://www.sacred-texts. com/bud/sbe10/sbe1005.htm).

Statues of the Saints, Santa Fe, New Mexico; courtesy of the author

Sri Swami Satchidananda, *The Yoga Sutras of Patanjali* (Integral Yoga Publications 1978), 52.

SUTRA 1.32

Chaco Canyon, New Mexico; courtesy of the author

Jaganath Carrera, *Inside the Yoga Sutras*, 80.

SUTRA 1.33

Temple Mural, Lumbini, Nepal; courtesy of the author

F. Max Muller, *The Dhammapada*, 53 (http://www.sacred-texts. com/bud/sbe10/sbe1017. htm).

SUTRAS 1.34–1.39 INTRODUCTION

Alan Watts, *The Essence of Alan Watts* (Celestial Arts 1974), 44.

James Haughton Woods, *The Yoga-System of Patanjali* (the Harvard University Press, 1914), 77.

SUTRA 1.34

On the Road to Taos Pueblo, Taos, New Mexico; courtesy of the author

Max Muller, *The Sacred Books of the East—The Upanishads*, (Oxford; The Clarendon Press, 1884) Svetasvatara Upanishad, Second Adhyaya, Verses 9-10 (http://www.sacred-texts.com/hin/ sbe15/sbe15007.htm).

SUTRA 1.35

Acoma Pueblo, New Mexico; courtesy of the author

Thich Nhat Hanh, *Art of Mindful Living—Tea Meditation* (http:// www.plumvillage.org/practice.html?start=23).

SUTRA 1.36

Blue Japanese Print #2; courtesy of Ken Adams

F. Max Muller, *The Sacred Books of the East—Svetasvatara Upanishad*, Fourth Adhyaya, Verses 18–20 (http://www.sacred-texts.com/hin/ sbe15/sbe15007.htm).

SUTRA 1.37

Cementerio de la Recoleta, Bueos Aires, Argentina; courtesy of the author

Ramakrishna poetically describes the nature of enlightened souls as follows:

"There is a fabled species of birds called Homa, which live so high in the heavens and so dearly love those regions that they never condescend to come down to earth. Even their eggs, which, when laid in the sky, begin to fall down to the earth attracted by gravity, are said to get hatched in the middle of their downward course and give birth to the young ones. The fledglings at once find out that they are falling down, and immediately change their course and begin to fly up towards their home, drawn thither by instinct. Men such as Suka Deva, Narada, Jesus, Samkarakarya and others, are like those birds, who even in their boyhood give up all attachments to the things of this world and betake them-selves to the highest regions of true Knowledge and Divine Light."

F. Max Muller, *Ramakrishna—His Life and Sayings* (http://www.sacred-texts.com/ hin/rls/index.htm).

SUTRA 1.38

Reclining Buddha, Luang Prabang, Laos; permission by Shutterstock

Ramana Maharshi, *Talks with Sri Ramana Maharshi* (Sri Ramanasramam, Tiruvannamalai, 1955), 286.

SUTRA 1.39

Temple Mural, Lumbini, Nepal; courtesy of the author courtesy of the author

"[To remove the obstacles] you could try a form of meditation that makes use of a visual object. For example, you can visualize something and then reflect on what it means to you. In India, we often meditate like this on the images of the gods. As we visualize a particular god in the mind's eye, we recite his or her name 108 or 1008 times, if we are following the tradition. We immerse ourselves about the god written by our great poets; we call the god over and over again by name. This kind of meditation helps the mind to become quieter and more clear and prepares us for dhyana, the merging of the ego with the object of meditation. We do nothing except focus our attention on the god. If you try this technique you should be sure that you use objects that will actually bring peace to your mind and spirit, not ones that will cause more distraction."

T. K. V. Desikachar, *The Heart of Yoga*, 128.

INTRODUCTION TO SUTRAS 1.40–1.47

Eknath Easwaran, *The Upanishads*, 111.

Eknath Easwaran, *The Upanishads*, 239.

Sri Swami Satchidananda, The Yoga Sutras of Patanjali, 64.

SUTRA 1.40

Barred Spiral Galaxy NGC 1300. Credit: NASA, ESA, and the Hubble Heritage Team (STScI/AURA)

Sri Swami Vivekananda, *Patanjali Yoga Sutras—Sanskrit Text with Transliteration, Translation, and Commentary* (Publisher Unknown), 44.

SUTRA 1.41

Humayun's Tomb, New Delhi, India; courtesy of the author

Swami Krishnananda, *The Study and Practice of Yoga*, Part I, Chapter 44.

SUTRA 1.42

Apples; courtesy of the author

Baba Hari Dass, *Fire Without Fuel*, 181.

SUTRA 1.43

Unknown artist, Yoru no shubi no matsu (Shubi Pine); Library of Congress Digital Archives, 1900

"The dharma of Thusness is intimately transmitted by Buddhas and ancestors. Now you have it; preserve it well. A silver bowl filled with snow; a heron hidden in the moon. Taken as similar, they are not the same; not distinguished, their places are known. The meaning does not reside in the words, but a pivotal moment brings it forth. Move and you are trapped, miss and you fall into doubt and vacillation. Turning away and touching are both wrong, for it is like a massive fire. Just to portray it in literary form is to stain it with defilement. In darkest night it is perfectly clear; in the light of dawn it is hidden. Like facing a precious mirror: form and reflection hold each other. You are not it, but in truth it is you."

Ch'an Master Tung-shan Liang-chieh, *The Song of the Precious Jeweled Mirror Samadhi* (translation by Toshu John Neatrour, Sheng-yen, and Kazu Tanahashi) http://www.sacred-texts.com/bud/zen/hz/hz.htm.

SUTRA 1.44

Ine ni inabikari, (Thunder and lightning over rice grain), Artist unknown; Library of Congress Digital Archives, 1890–1910

Lao Tzu, *Tao Te Ching,* A New Translation by Gia-Fu Feng and Jane English (New York: Vintage Books, 1972).

SUTRA 1.45

Periche, Nepal; courtesy of the author

The Yoga Aphorisms of Patanjai (Vedanta Society of Southern California 1953), 48–49.

SUTRA 1.46

Autumn leaves kaleidoscope; permission by Shutterstock

The Yoga Aphorisms of Patanjai, (Vedanta Society of Southern California 1953), 49.

SUTRA 1.47

Pumori, Nepal; courtesy of the author

Ken Wilber, *The Simple Feeling of Being,* 243.

INTRODUCTION TO SUTRAS 1.48–1.51

Eknath Easwaran, *The Upanishads,* 116.

Sri Swami Satchidananda, *The Yoga Sutras of Patanjali,* 74.

SUTRA 1.48

Borobudur, Java, Indonesia; courtesy of the author

"Yet, meditation will truly calm the mind, fill the heart with joy and bring peace to the soul; the serenity and joy last through-out the day and throughout your life. Meditation is not a simple diversion which works only as long as you are actively engaged in it. Meditation is not a pill which quickly wears off and carries unpleasant side-effects. Rather, meditation brings you into contact with God; it changes the very nature of your being. It brings you back to the world from which you come: the realm of the divine. As you sit in meditation you will realize the insignificance of that which causes anxiety; you will realize the transient nature of all your troubles. You will realize the infinite joy and boundless peace that comes from God."

Swami Chidanand Saraswati, *Drops of Nectar*, 178–179.

SUTRA 1.49

The Flower Buddha; permission of Shutterstock

Ekai, *The Gateless Gate, Buddha Twirls a Flower*, translation by Nyogen Senzaki and Paul Reps (London: John Murray, 1934).

SUTRA 1.50

Moon over Mount Inaba, (A warrior climbing Mount Inaba by the light of a full moon), Yoshitoshi Taiso; Library of Congress Digital Archives, 1888

"The impression that results from the samadhi by which you get ritambhara prajna will obstruct all other impressions. Everything dies away and there is no more coming back as an ordinary person, ignorant of your true nature. When you come to this stage, you always retain this knowledge. In this state you become a jivanmukta, a realized saint. "Jivan" means one who lives; "mukta" means liberated. So such a person is a liberated living being. You live, eat, and talk like anybody else, even do business like anybody else, but still you are liberated. A jivanmukta may be doing anything. He or she need not be sitting in samadhi in some cave; this person may be in Times Square, but is still a jivanmukta. A jivanmukta is involved in the world for the sake of humanity without any personal attachment."

Sri Swami Satchidananda, *The Yoga Sutras of Patanjali*, 75.

SUTRA 1.51

Kojima Island, Artist unknown; Library of Congress Digital
Archives, 1890-1920

"Last, is Samadhi. Divine Union. Ecstasy. Bliss. Samadhi literally
means to merge. To come together. Here the subject is completely
lost. The object is completely lost. There are no boundaries. No
barriers. No separation. The lover and the beloved become one.
Every cell of our being becomes saturated with God. We are no longer looking for Him or praying to Him. Rather we merge into Him
like the rain drop merges into the ocean. All identity is lost. We are
one with the source. When we attain Samadhi, our lives become
peaceful, joyful, problem free. Obstacles still come, but we are not
affected by them. Ups and downs are there in life, but we do not
go up and down. Samadhi is the divine shock-absorber. No matter
how rough the road of life may be, we are smooth and shock-free.
Samadhi means, essentially, that our lives are lived in peace, not in
pieces, and that is the ultimate goal of yoga-Divine Union."

H. H. Pujya Swami Chidanand Saraswatiji, *Yoga, The Essence of
Life* (Parmarth Niketan Ashram), 15.

AFTERWORD TO PADA ONE

Ramana Maharshi, *Talks with Sri Ramana Maharshi*, Talk 465,
455.

Chaumukha Temple (Jain temple), Ranakpur, India; courtesy of
the author

PADA TWO: SADHANA PADA

INTRODUCTION TO SUTRAS 2.1-2.11

Eknath Easwaran, *The Bhagavad Gita*, 207.

Sally Kempton, "Bouncing Back" (http://www.sallykempton.com/yjarticles/bouncing_art. html).

H. H. Pujya Swami Chidanand Saraswatiji, *Peace—For Us, For Our Families, For Our Communities and For the World* (Parmarth Niketan), 56.

SUTRA 2.1

Tamil Nadu, India (Image supporting Sutra 2.1), courtesy of the author

Sri Aurobindo, *The Future Evolution of Man* (Silver, Lake, Wisconsin: Lotus Press, 2003) (Quotation supporting Sutra 2.1)

Swayambhunath Temple, Nepal; (Image supporting tapas), courtesy of the author

Sri Swami Krishnananda, *The Yoga System,* 12 (Quotation supporting tapas)

Temple women; (Image supporting svadhyaya) permission by Shutterstock

Sri Swami Krishnananda, *The Yoga System*, 12 (Quotation supporting svadhyaya)

Buddha; (Image supporting Isvara pranidhanani), permission by Shutterstock

Sri Anandamayi Ma, *The Matri Vani,* Volume I, (Translated by Atmananda), Shree Shree Anandamayee Sangha Hardware, 1995) (Quotation supporting Isvara pranidhanani)

SUTRA 2.2

Udai Mandir Temple, Jodhpur, India; courtesy of the author

H. H. The Dalai Lama, *Transforming the Mind* (Thorsons Open Library, http://www.dalailama.com/teachings/training-the-mind.

SUTRA 2.3

Aztec Design, Mexico, permission by Shutterstock

"We do not know Universal Being. We know only the particular and the individual. We love and hate objects. We cling to life and fear death. The first mistake is to think, 'I am not the Universal'; the second to affirm, 'I am the particular'; the third to like certain things and to dislike others; the fourth to strive for perpetuating individuality by the instinct for self-preservation and self-reproduction. The error of forgetfulness of universality has produced affirmation of individuality, which has caused love and hate, or like and dislike, all which finally has led to desire for life and horror of death. This is our present state. We have now to wake up from this muddled thinking and go back to the truth of thinking universally. The union of the individual with the Universal is Yoga."

Sri Swami Krishnananda, *The Yoga System*, 6.

SUTRA 2.4

Temple Mural, Lumbini, Nepal; courtesy of the author

Baba Hari Dass, *Fire Without Fuel*, 156.

SUTRA 2.5

Yogyakarta, Indonesia, Candi Prambanan Hindu Temple; courtesy of the author

Swami Prabirthananda and Christopher Isherwood, *The Yoga Aphorisms of Patanjali, How to Know God, Translated With a New Commentary* (Vedanta Society of Southern California, 1953), 69.

SUTRA 2.6

Ranakpur, Rajasthan, India; courtesy of the author

Swami Prabirthananda and Christopher Isherwood, *The Yoga Aphorisms of Patanjali, How to Know God, Translated With a*

New Commentary (Vedanta Society of Southern California 1953), 66-67.

SUTRA 2.7

High-cast Hindus, Bombay, India; Library of Congress Digital Archives, 1922.

Ryokan, One Robe, *One Bowl—The Zen Poetry of Ryokan* (John Weatherhill, Inc. 1977), 28.

SUTRA 2.8

Market Woman, Yogyakarta, Indonesia; courtesy of the author

Third Ch'an Patriarch Chien-chih Seng-ts'an, *Faith Mind Inscription* (http://www.sacred-texts.com/bud/zen/fm/fm.htm), Verse 3.

SUTRA 2.9

Varanasi, India; courtesy of the author

Han-shan, *Cold Mountain—101 Chinese Poems*, translated by Burton Watson, Poem 74 (Boston, Massachusetts: Shambhala 1992), 102.

SUTRA 2.10

Big Sur, California; courtesy of the author

"In the music of the rushing stream sounds the joyful assurance, 'I shall become the sea.' It is not a vain assumption; it is true humility, for it is the truth. The river has no other alternative. On both sides of its banks it has numerous fields and forests, villages and towns; it can serve them in various ways, cleanse them and feed them, carry their produce from place to place. But it can have only partial relations with these, and however long it may linger among them it remains separate; it never can become a town or a forest.

But it can and does become the sea. The lesser moving water has its affinity with the great motionless water of the ocean. It moves through the thousand objects on its onward course, and its motion finds its finality when it reaches the sea. In the same manner, our soul can only become Brahma as the river can become the sea. Everything else she touches at one of her points, then leaves and moves on, but she never can leave Brahma and move beyond him. Once our soul realizes her ultimate object of repose in Brahma, all her movements acquire a purpose. It is this ocean of infinite rest which gives significance to endless activities."

Rabindranath Tagore, *Sadhana — The Realisation of Life* (New York: Macmillan Company, 1916), Chapter 8.

SUTRA 2.11

Image, Angkor Wat, Cambodia; courtesy of Jeffrey Siegel

Eknath Easwaran, The Bhagavad Gita, Chapter VI, 142.

INTRODUCTION TO SUTRAS 2.12–2.14

Ram Dass, *Still Here* (Riverhead Books, 2000), 28.

I. K. Taimni, *The Science of Yoga*, 144.

Swami Rajarshi Muni, *Yoga The Ultimate Spiritual Path*, 88.

Chaumukha Temple (Jain temple), Ranakpur, India; courtesy of the author

SUTRA 2.12

Koi under a Pine Branch, Maruyama, Okyo; Library of Congress, 1862

"Thus, the most important purpose and reason of rebirth is to attain liberation, to become one with God. People can go astray in one life. People can choose paths of passion instead of piety, paths of decadence instead of discrimination, and paths of hedonism instead of honor. Yet, God wants us all to come to Him. That is the purpose of human birth. So, He gives us more chances. We keep coming back until we learn the lessons of this human birth and until we transcend the limitations and temptations of the flesh. Thus, we must realize that everything we do which is not conducive to the path of God realization is simply an obstacle we are putting in our own way. Every act we commit which is not honest, divine and pure is simply one more stumbling block we put on our path. It is simply one more hurdle we will have to cross, if not this life then the next life."

H. H. Pujya Swami Chidanand Saraswatiji, *Drops of Nectar,* 47.

SUTRA 2.13

Esalen, Big Sur, California; courtesy of the author

Sri Swami Vivekananda, *Patanjali Yoga Sutras,* 67.

SUTRA 2.14

Megata, Matsu Pine; Library of Congress Digital Archives, 1870

"The king said: 'Why is it, Nagasena, that all men are not alike, but some are short-lived and some long-lived, some sickly and some healthy, some ugly and some beautiful, some without influence and some of great power, some poor and some wealthy, some low born and some high born, some stupid and some wise?'

The Elder replied: 'Why is it that all vegetables are not alike, but some sour, and some salt, and some pungent, and some acid, and some astringent, and some sweet?"

'I fancy, Sir, it is because they come from different kinds of seeds.'

'And just so, great king, are the differences you have mentioned among men to be explained. For it has been said by the Blessed One: "Beings, O Brahmin, have each their own Karma, are inheritors of Karma, belong to the tribe of their Karma, are relatives by Karma, have each their Karma as their protecting overlord. It is Karma that divides them up into low and high and the like divisions.' "

T. W. Rhys, David, *The Questions of King Milinda*, (Oxford: The Clarendon Press, 1890), 101.

INTRODUCTION TO SUTRAS 2.15–2.16

Eknath Easwaran, *The Bhagavad Gita*, 97.

Sri Swami Vivekananda, *Patanjali Yoga Sutras*, 69.

Grasshopper Eating Persimmon, Katsushika, Hokusai; Library of Congress Digital Archives, 1870–1900.

SUTRA 2.15

Borobudur, Java, Indonesia; courtesy of the author

Sri Swami Satchidananda, *The Yoga Sutras of Patanjali*, 100.

SUTRA 2.16

Dwarapala (The Giant Guardian) Plaosan Temple, Java, Indonesia; courtesy of the author

"What you should do is to learn the way of practice so you can identify your suffering, so you can recognize your suffering, you can look deeply into the nature of your suffering and you see the path leading to the cessation of suffering, and you should not endow yourself into looking for an ideology, a doctrine, a theory, you should not endow yourself into metaphysical speculations. This is very basic in the Buddhist teaching. The Buddha said, 'I only teach two things: I teach about suffering and the way out of suffering.' Your time should be devoted to the study and the practice of these two things. And when we are able to liberate ourselves from suffering, our mind becomes clear, then our mind can reflect ultimate reality without any intellectual searching. Your mind will become like a mirror that can reflect reality as it is, without any distortion."

Thich Nhat Hanh, *Eye of the Buddha Retreat: Discourse on the Ultimate Truth*, Tape Transcript 7 (http://www.plumvillage.org/dharma-talks/transcibe/227-discourse-on-the-absolute-truth-1.html).

INTRODUCTION TO SUTRAS 2.17–2.24

Eknath Easwaran, *The Upanishads*, The Mundaka Upanishad, 115.

Baba Hari Dass, *Fire Without Fuel*, 130.

Ian Whicher, *The Integrity of the Yoga Darsana* (State University of New York Press, 1998), 86.

Sri Swami Satchidananda, *The Yoga Sutras of Patanjali*, 103.

SUTRA 2.17

Holding Spirit Bow; courtesy of Ken Adams

Swami Vivekananda, *Patanjali Yoga Sutras*, 70.

SUTRA 2.18

Big Sur, California; courtesy of the author

Chaco Canyon, New Mexico; courtesy of the author

"The 'seen' is Nature or Prakriti (from the verb root, kr, "to make or do," and, pra, 'to bring forth). As the stuff of creation, it is the source of everything that becomes an object of perception for the Self. For the yogi, each and every event, whether marvelous or difficult to bear, is filled with meaning. Everything that happens is for the purpose of giving experiences to the Purusha. Or, more correctly, the experiences are for the mind, since the Purusha is by nature free. All Yoga theories and practices are for the sake of liberating the individual from the limitations of the ego and obscuring the power of ignorance. The 'experiences' mentioned in this sutra are learning experiences. They are the spiritual lessons that help turn our attention to the Self."

Jaganath Carrera, *Inside the Yoga Sutras*, 121-122.

SUTRA 2.19

Ropes; permission by Shutterstock

"The claim of the Sankhya philosophy is that beginning with the intellect, and coming down to a block of stone, all has come out of the same thing, only as finer or grosser states of existence. The Buddhi is the finest state of existence of the materials, and then comes Ahamkara, egoism, and next to the mind comes fine material, which they call Tanmatras, which cannot be seen, but which are inferred. These Tanmatras combine and become grosser, and finally produce this universe. The finer is the cause, and the grosser is the effect. It begins with the Buddhi, which is the finest material, and goes on becoming grosser and grosser, until it becomes this universe. According to the Sankhya philosophy, beyond the whole of this nature is the Purusa, which is not material at all. Purusa is not at all similar to anything else, either Buddhi, or mind, or the Tanmatras, or the gross material; it is not akin to any one of these, it is entirely separate, entirely different in its nature, and from this they argue that the Purusa must be immortal, because it is not the result of combination. That which is not the result of combination cannot die, these Purusas or Souls are infinite in number. Now we shall understand the aphorism, that the states of the qualities are defined, undefined, and signless. By the defined is meant the gross elements, which we can sense. By the undefined is meant the very fine materials, the Tanmatras, which cannot be sensed by ordinary men. If you practice Yoga, however, says Patanjali, after a while your perception will become so fine that you will actually see the Tanmatras."

Sri Swami Vivekananda, *Patanjali Yoga Sutras—Sanskrit Text With Transliteration, Translation and Commentary* (Publisher Unknown), 74.

SUTRA 2.20

NASA Space Observatories—Glimpse of faint afterglow of nearby stellar explosion; NASA, ESA, Hubble Heritage Team (STScI/ AURA)) (SPD-CHAND-photo/2005 /n132d/n132d.tif); 2005.

"I know the great Purusha, who is luminous, like the sun and beyond darkness. Only by knowing Him does one pass over death; there is no other way to the Supreme Goal. The whole universe is filled by Purusha, to who there is nothing superior, from who there is nothing different, from who there is nothing either smaller or greater; who stands alone, motionless as a tree, established in His own glory. That which is farthest from this world is without form and without affliction. They who know It become immortal; but others, indeed, suffer pain. He indeed is the great Purusha, the Lord of creation, preservation and destruction, who inspires the mind to attain the state of stainlessness."

The Principal Upanishads; translation and edited by Swami Nikhilananda; Svetasvatara Upanishad, (Dover Publications, 1963), Chapter III, Verses 8–10, 12.

SUTRA 2.21

Park Guell (Antoni Gaudi), Barcelona, Spain; courtesy of the author

Sri Swami Vivekananda, *Patanjali Yoga Sutras*, 79.

SUTRA 2.22

Varanasi, India; courtesy of the author

Sri Aurobindo describes the distinction between Purusha and Prakriti as follows:

"The distinction made in the Gita between the Purusha and the Prakriti gives us the clue to the various attitudes which the soul can adopt towards Nature in its movement towards perfect freedom and rule. The Purusha is, says the Gita, witness, upholder, source of the sanction, knower, lord, enjoyer; Prakriti executes, it is the active principle and must have an operation corresponding to the attitude of the Purusha. The soul may assume, if it wishes, the poise of the pure witness; it may look on at the action of Nature as a thing from which it stands apart; it watches, but does not itself participate. We have seen the importance of this quietistic capacity; it is the basis of the movement of withdrawal by which we can say of everything,— body, life, mental action, thought, sensation, emotion,—'This is Prakriti working in the life, mind and body, it is not myself, it is not even mine,' and thus come to the soul's separation from these things and to their quiescence."

Sri Aurobindo, *The Synthesis of Yoga* (Sri Aurobindo Ashram Publication Department, 1999), 431–432.

SUTRA 2.23

Water Drops; permission by Shutterstock

Eknath Easwaran, *The Bhagavad Gita*, 218.

SUTRA 2.24

Wall Mural, Albuquerque, New Mexico; courtesy of the author

"The 'experiencer' is the Atman, our real nature. The 'object of experience' is the totality of the apparent world, including the mind and the senses. In reality, the Atman alone exists, 'One without a second,' eternally free. But by the false identification through maya, which is the mystery of our present predicament, the Atman is mistaken for the individual ego, subject to all the thought-waves which arise and trouble the mind. That is why we imagine that we are 'unhappy' or 'happy', 'angry' or "lustful'. So long as the experiencer is falsely identified with the object of experience, we cannot know the Atman, our real nature. We remain in bondage, believing ourselves to be the slaves of experience."

Swami Prabirthananda and Christopher Isherwood, *How to Know God*, 79–80.

INTRODUCTION TO SUTRAS 2.25–2.27

Sri Swami Vivekananda, *Patanjali Yoga Sutras*, 82.

Jaganath Carrera, *Inside the Yoga Sutras*, 126.

SUTRA 2.25

Park Guell (Antonio Gaudi), Barcelona, Spain; courtesy of the author

Jaganath Carrera, *Inside the Yoga Sutras*, 125.

SUTRA 2.26

Tibet; courtesy of the author

Thikse Gompa, Ladakh, India; courtesy of the author

Sri Swami Vivekananda (http://www.vivekananda.org/quotes.aspx)

SUTRA 2.27

Stupas, Ladakh, India; courtesy of the author

Rizong Gompa, Ladakh, India; courtesy of the author

Rabindranath Tagore, *Gitanjali, Song Offerings*, Introduction by William Butler Yeats, 1913 (digireads.com, 2004).

INTRODUCTION TO SUTRAS 2.28–2.29

H. H. Pujya Swami Chidanand Saraswatiji, *Yoga, The Essence of Life*, 4.

SUTRA 2.28

Temple, Tamil Nadu, India ; courtesy of the author

Baba Hari Dass, *Fire Without Fuel*, 98.

SUTRA 2.29

Fractal Image of the Eight Limbs of Yoga; courtesy of the author

Jaganath Carrera, *Inside the Yoga Sutras*, 129.

INTRODUCTION TO SUTRAS 2.30–2.34

Sri Swami Krishnananda, *The Study and Practice of Yoga*, Chapter 6.

Swami Jnaneshvara Bharati, *The Yoga Sutras*, "Commentary on Sutra 2.34" (http://www.swamij.com/yoga-sutras-23034.htm).

Wall Mural, Udaipur, India; courtesy of the author

SUTRA 2.30

Tibet Temple; courtesy of the author

Sri Swami Krishnananda, *The Study and Practice of Yoga*, 10.

SUTRA 2.31

 Ceiling in Topkapi Palace, Istanbul, Turkey; courtesy of the author

Swami Prabirthananda and Christopher Isherwood, *How to Know God*, 23.

SUTRA 2.32

Temple Mural, Lumbini, Nepal; courtesy of the author

H. H. Pujya Swami Chidanand Saraswatiji, *Yoga: The Essence of Life*, 8.

SUTRA 2.33

Buddha Tooth Relic Temple, Singapore; courtesy of the author

Baba Hari Dass, *Fire Without Fuel*, 84.

SUTRA 2.34

Konen, Uehara, Hato zu (Waves); Library of Congress Digital Archives, 1878–1940

Swami Vivekananda, *Patanjali Yoga Sutras*, 63.

INTRODUCTION TO SUTRAS 2.35–2.45

Mahatma Gandhi; permission of Gandhi Serve Foundation, Berlin, Germany

Sri Swami Krishnananda, *The Yoga System*, Chapter 5.

The Collected Works of Mahatma Gandhi, Volume 33 (GhandiServe Foundation, 135 (http://www.gandhiserve.org/cwmg/cwmg.html)

SUTRA 2.35

Man, Rajasthan, India; permission by Shutterstock

H. H. Pujya Swami Chidanand Saraswatiji, Y*oga: The Essence of Life*, 5.

SUTRA 2.36

Woman, Rajasthan, India; permission by Shutterstock

 Swami Prabirthananda and Christopher Isherwood, *How to Know God*, 94.

SUTRA 2.37

Women, Rajasthan, India; permission by Shutterstock

Swami Prabirthananda and Christopher Isherwood, *How to Know God*, 95.

SUTRA 2.38

Woman, Rajasthan, India; permission by Shutterstock

H. H. Pujya Swami Chidanand Saraswatiji, *Yoga: The Essence of Life*, 6-7.

SUTRA 2.39

Man, Rajasthan, India; permission by Shutterstock

H.H. Pujya Swami Chidanand Saraswatiji, *Yoga: The Essence of Life*, 7.

SUTRA 2.40

Woman, Rajasthan, India; permission by Shutterstock

H.H. Pujya Swami Chidanand Saraswatiji, *Yoga: The Essence of Life*, 8.

SUTRA 2.41

Woman, Varanasi, India; courtesy of the author

Swami Vivekananda, *Patanjali Yoga Sutras*, 91.

SUTRA 2.42

Temple Priest, Jodhpur, Rajasthan, India; courtesy of the author

Swami Prabirthananda and Christopher Isherwood, *How to Know God*, 97.

SUTRA 2.43

Women, Rajasthan, India; permission by Shutterstock

Sri Swami Krishnananda, *The Yoga System*, 12.

SUTRA 2.44

Temple Mural, Lumbini, Nepal; courtesy of the author

Sri Swami Satchidananda, *The Yoga Sutras of Patanjali*, 149.

SUTRA 2.45

Man, Rajasthan, India; permission by Shutterstock

Sri Swami Krishnananda, *The Yoga System*, 13.

INTRODUCTION TO SUTRAS 2.46–2.48

B. K. S. Iyengar (http://www.bksiyengar.com/)

SUTRA 2.46

Borobudur, Java, Indonesia; courtesy of the author

Sri Swami Krishnananda, *The Study and Practice of Yoga*, Chapter 7.

SUTRA 2.47

Borobudur, Java, Indonesia; courtesy of the author

T. K. V. Desikachar, *The Heart of Yoga*, 219.

SUTRA 2.48

Borobudur, Java, Indonesia; courtesy of the author

B. K. S. Iyengar, *The Tree of Yoga* (Boston, Massachusetts: Shambhala 1989), 55-56.

INTRODUCTION TO SUTRAS 2.49–2.53

H. H. Pujya Swami Chidanand Saraswatiji, *Yoga, The Essence of Life*, 12.

Sri Swami Satchidananda, *The Yoga Sutras of Patanjali*, 160.

SUTRA 2.49

Stupa and Prayer Flags, Boudhanath Stupa, Kathmandu, India; courtesy of the author

The Hatha Yoga Pradipika, translation by Pancham Sinh (Munshirm Manaharlal Pub. Pvt.Ltd., 1997)

SUTRA 2.50

Ama Dablam, Nepal; courtesy of the author

"It (the restraint of breath) is external in case there is no flow of breath after expiration. It is internal in case there is no flow of breath after inspiration. It is suppressed in fluctuation in case there is no flow of either kind (neither of expiration nor inspiration), as the result of a single effort to suppress both. Just as water dropped upon a very hot stone shrivels up where it falls, so both at once cease to be. And each of these three is regulated in space; each deals with a certain amount of space. Each is regulated in time; in other words, defined by a limitation to a certain number of moments. Each is regulated in number; the first rising up by so many inspirations and expirations. In the same manner, the second rising up of the checked vital current is measured by so many inspirations and expirations. Likewise the third. Similarly it is gentle in method; similarly it is moderate; similarly it is keen. Thus it is regulated by number. So then, practiced in these ways, it becomes protracted and subtle."

James Haughton Woods, *The Yoga-System of Patanjali*, (The Harvard University Press, 1914), 193.

SUTRA 2.51

Stupa and Prayer Flags, Tengboche, Nepal; courtesy of the author

T. K. V. Desikachar, *The Heart of Yoga, Developing a Personal Practice*, 227.

SUTRA 2.52

Ama Dablam, Nepal; courtesy of the author

James Haughton Woods, *The Yoga-System of Patanjali*, 196.

SUTRA 2.53

Oranges; permission by Shutterstock

Thich Nhat Hanh, "The Moment is Perfect," *Shambhala Sun* (May 2008).

INTRODUCTION TO SUTRAS 2.54–2.55

Eknath Easwaran, *The Bhagavad Gita*, 96.

Udai Mandir Temple, Jodhpur, India; courtesy of the author

SUTRA 2.54

Gekko, Ogata, Dragonfly and Pumpkin; Library of Congress Digital Archives, 1890.

James Haughton Woods, *The Yoga-System of Patanjali*, 197.

SUTRA 2.55

Parmarth Niketan, Rishikesh, India; courtesy of the author

"Know the Self to be sitting in the chariot, the body to be the chariot, the intellect (buddhi) the charioteer, and the mind the reins. The senses they call the horses, the objects of the senses their roads. He who has no understanding and whose mind (the reins) is never firmly held, his senses (horses) are unmanageable, like vicious horses of a charioteer. But he who has understanding and whose mind is always firmly held, his senses are under control, like good horses of a charioteer. He who has no understanding, who is unmindful and always impure, never reaches that place, but enters into the round of births. But he who has understanding, who is mindful and always pure, reaches indeed that place, from whence he is not born again. But he who has understanding for his charioteer, and who holds the reins of the mind, he reaches the end of his journey, and that is the highest place of Vishnu.

Beyond the senses there are the objects, beyond the objects there is the mind, beyond the mind there is the intellect, the Great Self is beyond the intellect. Beyond the Great there is the Undeveloped, beyond the Undeveloped there is the Person (Purusha). Beyond the Person there is nothing— this is the goal, the highest road. That Self is hidden in all beings and does not shine forth, but it is seen by subtle seers through their sharp and subtle intellect."

Max Muller, *The Sacred Books of the East,* Katha Upanishad, Chapter 1, Verses 3–12.

INTRODUCTION TO VIBHUTI PADA

Sri Swami Satchidananda, *The Yoga Sutras of Patanjali*, 169.

INTRODUCTION TO SUTRAS 3.1–3.5

I. K. Taimni, *The Science Of Yoga*, 254.

Udai Mandir Temple, Jodhpur, India; courtesy of the author

SUTRA 3.1

Park Guell (Antoni Gaudi), Barcelona, Spain; courtesy of the author

H. H. Pujya Swami Chidanand Saraswatiji, *Yoga, The Essence of Life*, 13.

SUTRA 3.2

Tsuglagkhang Complex (Dalai Lama Temple), Dharamsala, India; courtesy of the author

H. H. Pujya Swami Chidanand Saraswatiji, *Yoga, The Essence of Life*, 14

SUTRA 3.3

Seashell; permission by Shutterstock

Swami Prabirthananda and Christopher Isherwood, *How to Know God*, 113-114.

SUTRA 3.4

Alan Houser, When Friends Meet, Santa Fe, New Mexico; courtesy of the author

I. K. Taimni, *The Science Of Yoga*, 254.

SUTRA 3.5

Wall Mural, Albuquerque, New Mexico; courtesy of the author

Jaganath Carrera, *Inside the Yoga Sutras*, 168.

ABOUT LILALABS PUBLISHING LLC

Lilalabs Publishing LLC is an artisanal press that produces works in the wisdom traditions and law. We are exploring the space where art, wisdom, and technology intersect. We believe that modern technology is offering us an unprecedented opportunity to create, produce, market, and experience works in new and exciting ways. New platforms will allow us to produce experimental works that will enable our readers to read these writings from a new perspective and gain fresh insights.

We view ourselves as producers of books, as well as publishers, and are exploring new paradigms in creating and distributing books. We are exploring the meaning of the concept of a book as it becomes more and more like a shape shifting container for content rather than a static object. We assist authors writing in the wisdom traditions. Finally, we are inspired by and express the spirit of yoga in all of our activities at Lilalabs.

For more information about Lilalabs see our Website: www.lilalabs. com. Lilalabs Publishing LLC is located in Berkeley, California.

ABOUT THE DIGITAL VERSION OF THE YOGA SUTRAS

We are currently developing an electronic version of this book which will be distributed as an app on the Apple platform. The electronic version will illuminate the Sutras by a multimedia presentation. Each sutra will be presented in a layout that contains the Sanskrit text, an English translation, imagery that illuminates the sutra and commentary. Each layout will feature a chant of the sutra in Sanskrit by a sanskrit scholar so that the reader can experience the sutras as a living tradition.

For more information about Lilalabs Publishing LLC and the digital version of the book, see our website: www.lilalabs.com.

ABOUT THE COVER

Cover imagery based on the artwork of Katherine Warinner.
Website: www.katherinewarinner.com.
Design by Aufuldish & Warinner
Website: www.aufwar.com.

ABOUT THE AUTHOR

Gary Kissiah has been practicing Yoga since 2000. He has studied Yoga at Esalen Institute, Big Sur, California, Parmarth Niketan Ashram, Rishikesh, India, and Satchidananda Ashram, Buckingham, Virginia. He has a Certificate of Yoga Philosophy from the California Institute of Integral Studies, is a RYT 200, and teaches yoga philosophy, law and ethics for Yoga teacher training programs. Gary has spoken at Yoga Journal Live, Wanderlust Teacher Training Programs, Yoga Alliance Business of Yoga Conference, Santa Fe Yoga Festival, and the Texas Yoga Festival. Gary has practiced corporate and business law for over 20 years. He was a partner with Akin Gump Strauss Hauer & Feld, a large international law firm, and a senior attorney with Microsoft. Gary has his own law firm, and specializes in representing yoga studios, teachers, and wellness businesses. He has written the Light on Law series of books which provides legal and business resources for yoga and wellness businesses. He enjoys traveling, trail running, mountain climbing, and photography.

COPYRIGHT INFORMATION

Copyright @2015 by Lilalabs Publishing LLC

Printed and bound in China.

Published by Lilalabs Publishing LLC
Website: www.lilalabs.com

ISBN-10: 0615388442
ISBN-13: 978-0-615-38844-1